THE RITE OF WAR

THE RITE OF WAR

by

STAN WINDASS

BRASSEY'S DEFENCE PUBLISHERS
(a member of the Pergamon Group)

LONDON · OXFORD · WASHINGTON · NEW YORK
BEIJING · FRANKFURT · SÃO PAULO · SYDNEY · TOKYO · TORONTO

U.K. (Editorial)	Brassey's Defence Publishers, 24 Gray's Inn Road, London WC1X 8HR
(Orders)	Brassey's Defence Publishers, Headington Hill Hall, Oxford OX3 0BW, England
U.S.A. (Editorial)	Pergamon-Brassey's International Defense Publishers, 1340 Old Chain Bridge Road, McLean, Virginia 22101, U.S.A.
(Orders)	Pergamon Press, Maxwell House, Fairview Park, Elmsford, New York 10523, U.S.A.
PEOPLE'S REPUBLIC OF CHINA	Pergamon Press, Qianmen Hotel, Beijing, People's Republic of China
FEDERAL REPUBLIC OF GERMANY	Pergamon Press, Hammerweg 6, D-6242 Kronberg, Federal Republic of Germany
BRAZIL	Pergamon Editora, Rua Eça de Queiros, 346, CEP 04011, São Paulo, Brazil
AUSTRALIA	Pergamon-Brassey's Defence Publishers, P.O. Box 544, Potts Point, N.S.W. 2011, Australia
JAPAN	Pergamon Press, 8th Floor, Matsuoka Central Building, 1-7-1 Nishishinjuku, Shinjuku-ku, Tokyo 160, Japan
CANADA	Pergamon Press Canada, Suite 104, 150 Consumers Road, Willowdale, Ontario M2J 1P9, Canada

First edition 1986

Library of Congress Cataloging in Publication Data
Windass, Stan, 1930–
The rite of war.
1. War.   2. World politics — 1945–   .   3. Europe —
Defenses.   4. World War III.   I. Title.
U21.2.W55   1986   355'.033'004   86–17039

British Library Cataloguing in Publication Data
Windass, Stan
The rite of war.
1. Military policy   2. International relations   3. World
politics — 1985–1995
I. Title
355'.0332   UA11

ISBN 0–08–033605–1

Printed in Great Britain by A. Wheaton & Co. Ltd., Exeter

Preface

The views presented in the following mock trial with which this book commences are necessarily simplified and stereotyped on both sides. Readers will be aware of the broad divergency of views in the West about relative 'blame' for the military confrontation which overshadows the world. In fact, a certain divergency of views, less broad and less explicitly expressed, but nonetheless significant, is perceptible in the East as well. The thesis of shared responsibility for world peace is gaining ground in the East as in the West. Nevertheless, there is an element of stylised ritual about the public exchange of boasts and insults between East and West; and it is a ritual which is quite familiar to anyone who has come into contact with the age-old traditions of human warfare. Boasts and insults prior to battle have always been an integral part of the game; and accusations of deceit and treachery levelled at the enemy are as familiar in the Germanic tradition as they are in the Old Testament — a fact which could hardly surprise anyone who remembers the saying of Sun Tzu, 'Deceit is the very essence of warfare.'

The purpose of this mock drama is not to reflect the subtleties of view on either side, but nor is it to suggest that each side has a similar case. Clearly the role of the military in the Soviet Union is much more predominant than the role of the military in the USA, and there is no comparison between the free and diverse association of peoples which constitutes the Western Alliance and the centralised alliance of Russian client states in Eastern Europe. The threat posed in Central Europe to Western Europe is massive and inescapable, and is in no way paralleled by a NATO threat to Eastern Europe.

However, in order to achieve a resolution of our security dilemma at this crucial point in human history, it is essential to understand that there are other ways of looking at the world than the ones we are used to. We need bifocal lenses to get at the truth in all its dimensions. Readers are invited to try these bifocals for size and to shop around elsewhere if they don't fit.

Contents

Chapter 1. You The Jury

Chapter 2. The Defence of Europe

Chapter 3. Ritualising Nuclear Weapons: I. Strategic

Chapter 4. Ritualising Nuclear Weapons: II. Battlefield and Intermediate

Chapter 5. The Rite of War

The charge — imperialism

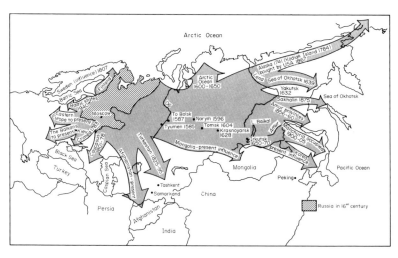

Soviet expansion and influence since the sixteenth century

1

You The Jury

The Charge: Imperialism

The charge, ladies and gentlemen, which is brought by these two protagonists against each other is that of *Imperialism*. Each accuses the other of seeking to construct a world empire by force. This implies that the accused are guilty of a systematic and sustained denial of the principle of the freedom and self-determination of peoples which is the foundation stone of international law, of the UN Charter, and of the Universal Declaration of Human Rights.

We shall hear the arguments of the two contestants in due order, and then ask the jury to pronounce a verdict.

Soviet Expansionism to 1945 — Prosecution

Accused: The Soviet Union.

Case for the Prosecution:

Before 1945, when the Cold War began, Russia (now disguised as the Soviet Union) had a long and consistent history of military expansionism. This tradition continues.

Russia has been an expansionist military power at least since the time of the Czar Ivan the Terrible in the sixteenth century. To realise this it is only necessary to look at the succession of maps of Russia at appropriate historical intervals. At the beginning of the reign of Ivan the Terrible, Russia was a modest-sized principality based on Moscow and about the size of England. Ever since then it has grown relentlessly, with only periodic setbacks which are always later restored. The expansion goes in all directions — westwards towards the Baltic, to give

1

'access' to the West by the subjugation of countries like Poland, Lithuania, Finland, Sweden and Denmark; southwards, to give 'access' to the Black Sea and the Caspian Sea, by conquest of the northern parts of the Turkish empire and the subjugation of Georgia; eastwards, first to the Urals, and then across the vast Steppes of Siberia towards the Pacific, presumably to secure access there as well.

Such expansion carried out consistently over a period of four centuries does not happen without a consistent dream or aspiration — or without a formidable and highly organised fighting force and system of military government. It is not surprising, therefore, that the role of the military has always been absolutely central in Russian society.

Of course there is always a great sense of 'mission' which goes with military empire, as we well know. The great dream of the Russians, going right back to Ivan the Terrible, was to be the 'Third Rome' — conquering and absorbing the second Rome in Constantinople, dominating the whole of the East and Asia through its natural affinity with Eastern people, while retaining also the imperial mantle of Rome in the West — a good recipe indeed for eventual world domination.

The expansion eastwards into Siberia from the seventeenth century onwards was a particularly breathtaking and bloodthirsty affair. The conquest was carried out on a 'twin-track' basis — partly commercial, partly military. Commercially, the driving force was the fur trade, and the unlimited greed of the Russian colonists. Militarily, the driving force was the Cossacks, who were roving bands of legalised marauders who accompanied the fur traders, set up frontier posts, subjugated the people and exacted tribute from them — usually in the form of fur. Any resistance was met with the utmost savagery. The legendary fall of Guigudar in 1651 is a case in point. This little town had formerly paid tribute to China. It contained 1000 souls. It was surprised at night and bombarded by the great Russian Cossack hero Khabarof. In the morning the entire population was slaughtered. According to popular accounts, the shouts of the Cossacks, whose bloodthirsty appetites had been whetted by a night of excitement and fighting, were drowned by the cries of the children and women as they were being butchered and dragged into the arms of the Cossacks whose hands were dripping with the blood of fathers, husbands and brothers.

This Russian drive to the east by no means came to a halt at the

Pacific coast. In the eighteenth and nineteenth centuries Moscow was staking out an empire in the Pacific and on the west coast of North America. Alaska, in fact, became a Russian territory. It is not hard to see that the only limit ultimately to Russian expansionism was the road block provided by a vigorous and growing USA in the east.

About the end of the nineteenth century, Russia's historical tendency to expand seemed to have come to an end. The boundaries to the east, west and south seemed to be roughly agreed. This was, however, an illusion. Early in the twentieth century Russia waged war against Japan with the aim of getting overlordship of Manchuria and Korea; and soon after the beginning of World War I she announced a 'peace plan' which would give her a big slice of Asiatic Turkey (not to mention Eastern Galicia and the Dardanelles).

I think the record of the accused speaks for itself. Much is made of the great Communist Revolution in 1917 which was something quite new. In fact, after World War I the Marxist–Leninist creed of the universal expansion of Communism gave a tremendous impetus to Russian expansionism — an impetus which has never been lost. The activities of the Russian-dominated Comintern in the immediate aftermath of World War I were clearly aimed at establishing control over Germany, and in 1939 Stalin made an agreement with Nazi Germany to partition Poland between the two of them.

We have now learnt from long and bitter experience that 1917 only marked a brief pause, and that the heirs of the Czar's expanding military empire soon renewed their traditional march which continues to this day.

Soviet Expansionism to 1945 — Defence

Defendant: The Soviet Union.

Case for the Defence:

The expansion of Czarist Russia until the Revolution in 1917 was different from that of other European powers in that it was more benign. The revolutionary government in 1917 totally rejected all concepts of empire.

The rigmarole with which we have been presented by our accuser is remarkable for its total lack of historical common sense and perspective.

Anyone with the slightest understanding of history will know that the processes by which Russia grew were similar in most respects to the processes by which other European powers grow.

This expansion took various forms. First of all, way back in the sixteenth and seventeenth centuries, a number of little principalities in Central Russia were united around the Duchy of Moscow — won back for the most part from alien rule by Poland and Lithuania. This is exactly what happened when France was unified around the domain of the kings in the 'Ile de France' in Paris, when Spain was united round Castille and Aragon, Italy around Piedmont, or Germany around Brandenburg-Prussia. In some cases conquest was involved, but more usually voluntary grouping together — as when the Ukraine revolted against Poland and joined up with the Russian Czar for protection.

At a later stage, these power centres grew by drawing in backward nations — as in the Caucasus, Central Asia and the Far East. That was very similar to the way other European countries built up their vast empires — like England, France, Spain and Portugal. The main difference was that the Russians absorbed their *neighbours*, to whom they had close natural ties, whereas the other European powers carved up Africa and the Far East and subjected the whole peoples to alien rule.

A further development was a great expansion into almost uninhabited land — in the Russian case, across Siberia to the Pacific Ocean. Of course Russian expansion to the east at that time shared much of the evils of American expansionism to the west. The Russian explorers were motivated by greed just as the Americans were. They wanted to make more money out of furs, animal hides and minerals just like the American pioneers. Like the Americans, the Russians spread out into vast thinly populated regions, inhabited largely by nomads — Indians in North America, Asian tribesmen, or Siberians.

The main difference is that the Asian tribesman survived, and the American Indian did not. The Russians subordinated the tribesmen and made them into fur collectors; the Americans killed off the Indians and stole their land. The contrast today is between the pathetic remnant of Indians in North America confined to their 'reservations' and the thriving Central Asian Republic which now enjoy all the advantages of Soviet civilisation without any class distinction.

The second point about Siberia is this. Just look at a map. There is no natural barrier or frontier between Moscow and the Pacific. Imagine what it was like living in Russia before its expansion with that open doorway to the east. Remember also that the whole of this vast area to the east was overrun by Mongolia in the Middle Ages and the whole of Russia was threatened and dominated for centuries by Tatars who attacked from the east and forced Russian people to pay tribute to the 'Great Khan', submitting the Russian people to alien military rule, while they were simultaneously attacked by enemies to the west — namely Poland and Lithuania. The Moscow Czars really only became the power centre of modern Russia by standing up against and defeating and eventually repelling their Tatar oppressors and regaining lost lands. In the light of this, it is hardly surprising that Russia should have wanted to secure its eastern and western frontiers — and that meant expanding eastward and westward. The Americans, on the other hand, could hardly claim defence as a reason for killing off the Indians, and have no experience of attack either from east or west.

Yes. Russia acquired control of a large adjacent area between 1853 and 1914. But, between the same years, Great Britain, France, Germany, Italy and Belgium partitioned among themselves the entire continent of Africa. The Belgian share of Africa, the so-called Belgian Congo, was approximately as large as the totality of the Russian acquisitions between 1853 and 1914, and the share of France, 3.5 million square miles, was approximately four times larger.

The revolution in 1917, however, marked a complete break with the past. It is historical nonsense to say that the new Communist regime continued in the imperial tradition of the Czars. The principle of equal rights and self-determination of all people and nationalities was fundamental to the revolutionary ideal. It was both believed in and acted upon. Take border states for instance. In 1907 the Russian state had made an agreement with England to carve up Persia between them. This agreement was scrapped. At the same time all the Russian 'protectorates' were abolished, and all commercial privileges over Asiatic peoples were renounced. New treaties as between equals were made with Persia, Afghanistan, Mongolia and Turkey in 1921. Afghanistan accepted Soviet aid against Britain. None of these countries became subordinate to Russia or were incorporated in the USSR.

Georgia, Armenia and Azerbaydzhan were formed into the independent Trans-Caucasian Republic, which freely joined the USSR in 1922. As regards the peoples who were part of Russia at the time of the Revolution, the right of self-determination was accorded to them also. Indeed, the right of self-determination for all nationalities — which includes the right to independence — is written into the constitution of the USSR.

What happened in fact after the Russian Revolution is that anti-Russian groups, supported by the Western imperialism, took over power in the former Russian territories of Finland, Latvia, Estonia and Lithuania, and Poland acquired a large slice of Russian territory. By a humiliating peace treaty in 1918 (the Treaty of Brest-Litovsk) the Western powers succeeded in shrinking Russia by 1.25 million square miles, with a loss of 62 million people, 32 per cent of her factories and 26 per cent of her railroad. This insidious attack on the integrity of our people left a deep scar which has yet to be healed.

US Expansionism to 1945 — Prosecution

Accused: The USA.

Case for the Prosecution:

The USA, from its foundation up to 1945, exhibited all the traits of European colonialism, and advanced steadily from domination of a continent to domination of a hemisphere and then to aspirations of world empire.

The thirteen American colonies which won independence from Britain in 1776 were only a small country, but they were true heirs to European imperialism and had boundless ambitions. The expansion to the west, to the north and to the south was like an explosion, and just as destructive to native peoples and neighbouring states. The main motive for expansion was greed, trafficking in land, timber and furs. To the south was the Spanish empire, from which Florida was 'acquired' by a so-called 'purchase' in 1819. To the south-west was Mexico, from which the USA tried to 'buy' California and New Mexico — and when Mexico refused they went to war, occupied Mexico City, and forced them to cede Florida and New Mexico. To the north, Canada was in the way, and this the USA sought repeatedly but less successfully to acquire by guile or by force.

During this period the myth developed of the 'manifest' destiny of the USA to take possession of the whole of the entire continent — indeed perhaps of the whole hemisphere. Americans are still brought up on the myth that they 'discovered' the continent — as if there was nobody there before! It's like a car thief saying he 'discovered' someone's car. At least Russia was free from this kind of hypocrisy.

The so-called 'Monroe Doctrine', proclaimed by President Monroe of the USA in 1823, was nothing else than a claim to imperial power by the USA over both American continents. It amounted to the greatest effective claim to empire ever made in the history of humanity. There was to be 'no further European colonisation in the New World, no intervention by European goverments, and no transfer of any European colonies from one European sovereign to another'. No intervention, in other words, from anyone in the other hemisphere. The USA therefore had exclusive rights. An empire of half the world.

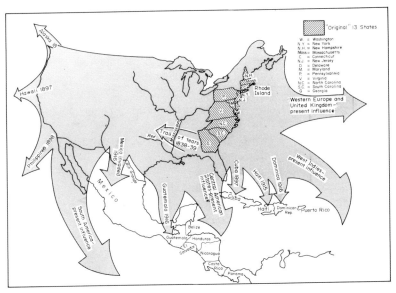

US expansion and influence since the sixteenth century

In its vast expansion westward, the American treatment of the native Indian people was one of the great crimes against human rights of recent world history — a crime which, as we know, still haunts the conscience of right-thinking Americans. We need only mention one event to recall the horrors of that period — the eviction of the Cherokees in 1838. The Cherokee was a proud and competent people who had in 1827 adopted a constitution on the US model and claimed sovereign status. This was of no avail — 'Equal dignity and rights' did not apply to Indians. They were callously rounded up like so many cattle, men, women and children, uprooted, marched off to distant and unknown lands, swept away like so much human refuse to clear the land up to the Mississippi for the 'new civilisation'. Many committed suicide rather than leave the land where the bones of their ancestors were buried. At a later date the Indians of the Great Plains to the west were pursued and hunted down like wild animals. Their treatment was justified by some because they were 'lower races' — perhaps descendants of the Canaanites expelled by Joshua. Like all military empires, the Americans developed their own theory of a master race which justified their conquests and their brutality.

The Americans' attitude to the indigenous peoples, or 'Indians', is recorded indelibly in their everlasting 'cowboy' and 'Indians' folklore; and they now try to make the Russians their Indians.

When the Americans arrived at the west coast they met up with the Russians who also expanded their settlements across the continent of Asia and into Alaska. In some ways it could be said that the Americans met up on the west coast with their mirror image. This is not to say, of course, that the thrust for expansion ended at the coast. By no means. The hemisphere over which the Americans claimed rule by manifest destiny apparently included the Pacific as well. The independent kingdom of Hawaii was annexed in 1894, and the coastlands of China and Japan were subjected to an 'opening up' process. At the end of the nineteenth century, in 1898, it was the turn of the Philippines to be 'liberated'. The Philippines belonged to Spain at the time, and when the USA went to war with Spain a national liberation movement emerged, confident of US support. US forces did indeed arrive — but only to annexe the islands and inaugurate colonial rule in the face of bitter opposition from freedom fighters, leaving a legacy of social division and misrule which lasts to this day.

The Americans' colonisation of their 'homeland' was finalised by the Civil War, when the North defeated the South — allegedly on the grounds of slavery, but in fact to enforce the dominance of the North over territories which wished to secede. A new order was born from war and conquest — the south was the anvil on which capitalism forged its power.

Like a vulture, America preyed on the decaying Spanish Empire. Hawaii was annexed in 1894, Cuba came under US military occupation, Puerto Rico was absorbed. A pattern of periodic military interventions was established throughout the Caribbean and Central America, which gradually turned into American slave estates. Investment and economic exploitation went hand in hand with periodic military interventions. In 1915 Haiti was forced to submit to US control, military control over Santo Domingo was established in 1916, and Nicaragua had to sign a treaty in 1916 accepting US ascendancy. Mexico was invaded in 1916. Guatemala became the first 'banana republic', with the United Fruit Company controlling all railways and most of the fertile land.

During World War I, 1914–1918, America for a while stood aloof. It still confined its expansionist ambitions to one hemisphere, and pretended to be above the sordid squabbles of the Old World. However, during the war American ambitions began to grow. Some Americans began to see that by linking up with the vast and farflung British Empire they could claim world hegemony. At the same time they feared the commercial rivalry of Germany. It was at this time that the idea of the mystical vocation of the Anglo-Saxon race began to take shape — the idea that the English-speaking people were the new chosen race, who would confer order upon the world. In 1917 the USA entered the war and so became thoroughly embroiled in Europe in time to enjoy the victory (and incidentally to enjoy a doubling of their GNP). Britain was by no means backward in wooing back the USA into the old imperialist fold — not the least because she felt the need for a prop as her own power declined.

Some farsighted Americans already saw a step further ahead, when the USA would inherit from Britain the mantle of world domination. Britannia would not 'rule the waves' for ever. The great British writer D. H. Lawrence wrote in 1923 that 'America, that extremist in world assimilation and world one-ness, is reacting into a violent egocentricity, a truly American egocentricity. As sure as fate we are on the brink of universal American Empire.'

At the beginning of World War II in Europe America also held back, preferring to work through her proxy Great Britain and confine herself to 'lease-lend' economic aid. As Goebbels correctly put it, 'America will fight to the last Englishman.' What drew America inevitably into the war, however, was a double challenge to growing American power. On the one hand, there was Germany, which was getting just too ambitious, and was beginning to appear as a menace to American rights both in the Atlantic and the Pacific Oceans. On the other hand, there was Japan, which was busy trying to conquer China and looked like setting up an empire in the East even more threatening to American imperialism than the German empire in Europe. Though there was still a part of the American power élite which wanted to subdue Japan by 'dollar diplomacy', it was clear that America would from now on have to fight for its empire in a big way, and the Japanese clinched the decision by attacking the US Fleet in Pearl Harbor.

The US entry into the war marked the beginning of the final phase of American military imperialism. But that is a story we must pick up later on.

US Expansionism to 1945 — Defence

The Declaration of Independence (1776) lays down the basic principles on which American society is founded. All men, it declares, are created equal, and endowed by their creator with certain inalienable rights — among these are life, liberty, and the pursuit of happiness. To secure these rights (and only to secure these rights), governments are instituted among men, deriving their just powers from the consent of the governed; and when any form of government becomes destructive of these ends, it is the right of the people to alter or abolish it.

No-one's history is unblemished; but throughout the two centuries since its foundation, the USA has never let go of the great vision that was expressed in the Declaration of Independence. Nobody would deny the horrors of slavery, or the excesses of the Indian War. But let us also remember that the Civil War, which was the most traumatic event in our history, was fought for the liberation of slaves, and since that time the liberated black people of the USA have asserted and won the full rights to equality which are guaranteed by the constitution of their country.

As regards expansionism, however, let us get our history into perspective. The subsequent Mexican War (1846–48) was not a war sought by the USA; it was caused by the refusal of Mexico to accept the independence of Texas. Texas, which had been part of the Mexican empire, became a free and independent republic after the great victory of San Houston in 1836, and later Texas joined up with the USA. The subsequent war against Mexico lasted little over a year, since the Mexican empire was clearly crumbling. After the fall of Mexico City, the USA negotiated a purchase of largely uninhabited territories in the south-west of the USA, which are now the prosperous states of New Mexico, California, Nevada, Utah and Arizona.

It is a scandalous misrepresentation of history to depict America's reluctant entry into World War I in 1917 as having anything at all to do with expansionist aims. It is well known that President Wilson throughout the first part of that war did everything in his power to act as a mediator between the warring European powers — seeking to achieve what he called 'peace without victory'. It was only when the aggressive and expansionist intentions of Germany became clear beyond doubt that the USA was forced to intervene; indeed, the decision to go to war was only clinched when it was revealed that Germany was entering into a conspiracy with Mexico to detach Texas, Arizona, and New Mexico from the USA — and when three US merchant ships were attacked and sunk by German submarines.

At the end of the war, it was President Wilson who, in the tradition of the US Declaration of Independence, took the lead in trying to ensure that the peace treaty was based on the principle of the freedom of self-determination of peoples. It was also his initiative to launch the League of Nations, whose purpose was to ensure that every nation, however small, would enjoy the support of all others in the League against any aggressor. However much President Wilson might be maligned for excessive idealism, he was the carrier of a torch which was handed on from the founding fathers of the USA. His purpose was to establish a brotherhood of free people throughout the world, and that is still our steadfast aim.

American deep and lasting aversion to colonialism was also obvious at the end of World War I. The victorious Allies had to decide what to do about the empires of their defeated enemies. Having made such a fuss about 'self-determination', they could hardly just grab for themselves all colonies which had been ruled by Germany and the Austro-Hungarian imperialists. They therefore devised the respectable idea of 'mandates' — sharing out the old colonies among themselves to be 'looked after' until they grew up and became independent. Immense pressure was put on America to 'join the club' and take on mandates — Palestine, German East Africa, Armenia — but President Wilson would have none of it. His concern, in the true American tradition, was that all peoples should be free, and should form one family, in a world made safe for democracy by co-operation among the great powers. Far from attempting to consolidate its influence in Europe, the USA after World War I was largely concerned with internal development, and was only dragged reluctantly back into international conflict by the brutal attack of the Japanese on Pearl Harbor in 1941.

Throughout the entire period of American history there has been a firm refusal on the part of the people of the USA to have any truck with old world colonialism, or to maintain any standing army in times of peace. There could hardly be a greater contrast between the early development of the USA and the military expansionism of the Soviet Union, which we shall now further investigate.

'Preying like a vulture on the decaying Spanish Empire' is a very odd description of what actually occurred between Spain and the USA at the end of the nineteenth century. Let me remind my opponent of the historical facts.

Certainly the USA had become a great world power by the end of the century — but this was entirely because of the vitality of its people and the consequent flourishing of the US economy. Throughout this early period, people of the USA refused to have any truck with European colonialism, which they had totally rejected in the War of Independence — and they also refused to countenance the idea of maintaining a standing national army. This was, of course, at a time when Russia was already a vast military empire, depending on a massive standing army to maintain its power.

The USA was drawn into a brief war of liberation against Spanish rule in Cuba in 1898. Cuba, like Puerto Rico and the Philippines, was at that time part of the Spanish empire. In 1898 there was a popular rebellion in Cuba against Spanish rule, and terrible atrocities against the people were carried out by the Spanish colonial overlords. In the light of our deep belief in the freedom and equality of all men, we could hardly stand by and ignore the cries for help of the oppressed people of Cuba. Because of popular demand, we did indeed intervene in Cuba. The war lasted three months, and its only purpose was to secure Spanish withdrawal and the independence of Cuba.

As regards the Philippines, whatever the rights and wrongs of past history, our accuser omitted to mention that these islands were granted full independence in 1953, while Hawaii, of course, obtained full statehood in 1959.

Soviet Expansionism since World War II — Prosecution

Accused: The Soviet Union.

Case for the Prosecution:

After 1945 the Soviet Union continued its tradition of military expansion, trying to bring the whole of Europe into its sphere of influence, and establish puppet regimes throughout the Third World. It was only prevented from doing so by the resistance of the USA and the formation of NATO.

Cold War

At the end of the war in 1945 Stalin did all he could to push Russia's empire as far west as possible — preferably right to the Atlantic. There is no question at all that the very least Stalin wanted was to have 'subordinated' governments in Poland, Czechoslovakia and the Baltic states. He never even entertained the idea of allowing free and independent Eastern European states to be reconstituted. British Foreign Minister Anthony Eden reported a conversation with the Soviet ambassador in August 1943, in which the ambassador outlined just two options for a postwar settlement: either two 'spheres of influence' in Europe, one Russian and one American, or a kind of superpower condominium in Europe, with Russia and America having an equal say. The second option, the equal-right-to-intervene option, was greatly preferred by Soviet governments — because in view of Europe's weakness, and America's distance, equal rights to intervene was almost bound to lead to Russian domination of Europe — especially as Stalin knew what he was aiming at, and Roosevelt did not.

As it happened, Stalin had to make do with the lesser option — the sphere of influence. By the time the war ended in 1945, Russian troops were established in Poland, Czechoslovakia, the Balkans and East Germany — and they never left. A government 'friendly' to Moscow had been set up in Warsaw. Churchill and Roosevelt protested that they would not recognise the new Polish Government until free elections had been held — but the protest never found its way into the Yalta spheres of influence agreement, and although elections were never held, the new regime was soon accepted by the West. Moscow certainly won that round.

What is interesting about this military expansion of Russia into Eastern Europe is that it *very* closely matched the imperialist ambitions of the Czars. This can easily be verified by looking at imperial Russia's war aims in 1914 — at the beginning of World War I, and *before* the communists took over. These aims included extensive 'rectification of borders' in a westerly direction, and the 'weakening of Germany as the chief enemy of Slavdom and Russia'. They also included taking over Constantinople from Turkey. All these aims were followed to the letter in 1945 — including an attempt to take over part of Turkey. So much for the claim that Russia ceased to be a military empire all of a sudden in 1917.

The additional factor brought in by the communists was that ideological domination was added to military domination. Unlike Russia's Asian empire, the conquered Europeans in Poland, Czechoslovakia and the Balkan states had experience of real democracy and real elections. Stalin's view, however, was that 'whoever occupies a territory imposes on it his own social system'. That meant the one-party communist state in the Russian style. It's hardly an accident that every country occupied by Russia adopted this system — and that *no* country *not* occupied by Russia adopted it!

Having established its empire by military means in Eastern Europe, it soon became clear that Russia would hang on to it by military means if it was ever challenged. The two most obvious cases which shocked the world were the Russian intervention in Hungary in 1956 and in Czechoslovakia in 1968.

In Hungary, elections were in fact held in 1945 and in 1947 in which the Communists failed to gain a majority. However, the party, backed by the continuing presence of the Soviet Army, gradually seized control of all key posts and in 1949 eliminated all opposition parties, giving Hungary a Soviet-type constitution and a Soviet-style dictator, Rakosi. Opposition to the dictator led to a successful peoples' revolution in 1956. A new government was formed, political prisoners were released (including Cardinal Mindsenty), and Hungary proclaimed itself neutral, appealing to the United Nations for backing and guarantees. Within days, however, Soviet forces poured into the country. Many thousands were killed, 200,000 fled. Nagy was executed, and a pro-Russian puppet was installed.

In Czechoslovakia there was a similar story. Elections were held in 1946 in which the Communists failed to win a majority, and a coalition government was formed. But Communists, backed by the Soviet Army, seized all key positions and by 1948 had forced a one-party state. Denial of political freedom and economic decline again produced a rebellion of the people, this time within the Communist Party itself. In 1968 Dubcek, duly elected as Communist Party leader, introduced a programme of liberal reforms — including freedom of the press and more contacts with the West. As a result, Soviet troops, aided by East Germans, Bulgarians and Hungarians, invaded Czechoslovakia. In 1969 Dubcek was replaced by a pro-Russian dictator Husak, who cancelled all Dubcek's reforms.

Much more recently, we have seen Russian tanks rolling forward in other parts of the world. In 1979, Soviet forces invaded Afghanistan. Their immediate purpose was clearly to establish a puppet regime subservient to the Kremlin. There was no request for help from the Afghan goverment — indeed the Afghan leader was murdered by the invading forces; and there was certainly no welcome from the people. Seven years later there has been no withdrawal of Soviet occupancy forces, which now number over 100,000. In spite of ever-increasing use of armed forces, the Soviet Union has been quite unable to crush the resistance of a people fighting for freedom and self-determination. The Panshir Valley, where the fiercely independent tribesmen had their base, has been subject to saturation bombing. Every human habitation has been destroyed. When villages are entered by the Soviet forces and arms are found, every man, woman and child is killed. Yet still the fight for freedom continues.

Out of a total population of 15 million, 4 million Afghans have fled to Pakistan, 1.5 million to Iran, and 2 million are homeless. Thus half the population is in exile. In 1984 the UN General Assembly adopted a resolution which called on all parties concerned to withdraw foreign troops from Afghanistan, and create conditions in which refugees could return in safety. This resolution, building on the basic right of self-determination enshrined in the UN Charter, reaffirms the right of the Afghan people to determine their own form of government and to choose their economic, political and social system free from outside intervention, subversion, coercion or constraint of any kind whatsoever.

Russian policy in Afghanistan is a continuation of the age-old tradition of military expansionism. Since the time of the Czars, Russian leaders have pursued the dream of a warm water port on the Indian Ocean. Afghanistan in Soviet hands also presents a threat to the oil resources of the Middle East. Clearly the Soviet Union is seeking to add Afghanistan to its empire by military means, 'Sovietise' Afghan society, and effectively incorporate it in the USSR. Only the indomitable will of the Afghan people and the force of world public opinion stands in their way.

Finally, it is not just in Europe or on the border of the Soviet Union that we have to beware of Soviet expansionism.

It is the deliberate policy of the Soviet Union to intervene in internal conflicts in the Third World in order to expand their military and ideological empires. The rule seems to be wherever there is trouble, stir it up. Take Angola, for instance, in Southern Africa. It was once a Portuguese colony. The Soviets intervened in the independence struggle and managed to set up a Marxist–Leninist puppet government which is still totally dependent on Soviet and Cuban military personnel and so-called 'advisers'. This is obviously a clever system for getting a foothold in any country where there is social unrest. If it were allowed to continue, Russia could through such means build up a worldwide empire in this way with minimum effort. Angola is typical.

When we look at all the examples of Soviet military intervention world wide, since 1945, it is impossible to avoid the conclusion that, whatever the rhetoric, the imperialists still reign in the Kremlin, and it is only the resistance of the free world which can restrain the forces of domination.

Soviet Expansionism since World War II — Defence

Accused: The Soviet Union.

Case for the Defence:

The Soviet military presence in Eastern Europe has always been entirely for defence. Soviet military involvement elsewhere has always been strictly in accord with international law and at the invitation of friendly governments.

There are one or two considerations that the prosecution has neglected in his lurid and one-sided account of the beginning of the so-called 'Cold War' between East and West.

First of all, it is true that Russian troops remained in considerable numbers in Eastern Europe after they had destroyed Nazi Europe, and that we played a part in helping stable regimes to emerge from the chaos and devastation of war. What else might we have done? Just think for a moment about Russian history. Repeatedly Russia has been invaded from the west. In 1812 Napoleon burnt Moscow to the ground, in 1917 we were invaded by Western powers intent on destroying all the achievements of the Revolution, and finally, between 1941 and 1945, the Nazis devastated most of the USSR west of the Urals and killed 20 million Soviet citizens. There is hardly a family that has not lost close relatives in that terrible war.

What were we to do when we had destroyed the evil regime which was responsible? Withdraw and let it regenerate? What did the West expect? Well, as it happens, it was quite clear what the West expected, because it was agreed at Yalta by Stalin, Roosevelt and Churchill. No-one wanted a political chaos in Central Europe. That would have been a recipe for World War III. We agreed on spheres of influence, and Russia has never departed from the agreement. The idea that we are poised to invade the West is a pure fiction without any historical basis. Russia has invaded no state since it destroyed Hitler's empire. It is well known that we seek stability and non-intervention.

That is why we had regrettably to take police action in Hungary and

Czechoslovakia in 1956 and 1968. In both cases we were asked to intervene to counteract subversive forces backed by the West. We had good reason to fear that West Germany would take advantage of social unrest in these countries to overthrow the stable socialist governments and re-establish a hostile Germany in a way that would present an intolerable threat on the very borders of the Soviet Union, and throw away all that had been achieved in the Great Patriotic War.

It is false, however, to say that Socialism was imposed on Eastern Europe by the Soviet Union. National liberation movements were already strong in Eastern Europe, and socialism was strongly allied to these liberation movements — as indeed it still is. In Yugoslavia and in Albania the national liberation movements led directly to socialist governments which were clearly in accord with the aspirations of the people. In Hungary and Czechoslovakia there may not have been an overall socialist majority in the elections — but the Communists were certainly the largest party, and the only party able to form a stable government.

Finally, in relation to Afghanistan, it is also important to get the historical record straight.

Afghanistan is a poor, mountainous country which until 1973 had a long history of stable and friendly relations with the Soviet Union. In 1973 there was a coup in which the old king was deposed by his cousin (Daoud), and the USA saw a chance of drawing Afghanistan into its sphere of influence. The Shah of Iran sent in $2 billion of aid, and secret police. Afghan police were sent to the USA and West Germany for training.

As the USA had hoped, the regime moved to the right and started a 'purge' of so-called Communists. The policy backfired, however, because this purge led to a revolutionary uprising in which the US puppet government was withdrawn and a Communist goverment was successfully installed. This government was and is the only internationally recognised government in Afghanistan, and it was *at the invitation of this government that Soviet troops entered Afghanistan*. No-one disputes this fact, which would stand up before the International Court of Justice.

Of course we deeply regret the continuing instability in Afghanistan, which we cannot but see as a most serious threat to our national security. If the USA is so concerned about anti-American groups in Nicaragua, which is a thousand miles from the USA, imagine how we must regard anti-Soviet groups in neighbouring Afghanistan, groups which are being supported and armed by the USA with the largest covert military aid budget ever undertaken by the CIA. The US operation in Afghanistan is a dagger pointed at our back, and we in co-operation with the government of Afghanistan must defend ourselves. When the USA is prepared to commit itself to non-intervention in our 'backyard', then some accommodation will become possible.

In reply to the charge of Soviet expansionism, which the USA uses as a cover, we need only quote the 1980 report of the Foreign Affairs Committee of the British House of Commons on Afghanistan — a committee in which there was a Conservative majority. The report concluded that the Soviet intervention was a defensive measure and that the Committee 'heard no evidence that the invasion of Afghanistan was part of a grand strategy to extend its influence to the Gulf and threaten Western oil supplies'.

Our reasons for remaining in Afghanistan are not, however, just to be understood in terms of Soviet national interests. Our concern in Afghanistan, as elsewhere, is for justice and human rights.

What is the struggle in Afghanistan about? What does the new power want and what do the rebels want? In the old Afghanistan about 40,000 landlords owned 70% of the land. The overwhelming majority of peasants had no land. The new power has eliminated large-scale private landholding and given land to the peasants.

The new power has cancelled peasant debts and raised women from the status of household slave to equal rights. It is making rapid progress towards eliminating illiteracy (formerly 90–95 per cent) and is laying the foundations of a system of modern health care. In general, the new power is bent on social progress and social justice. And what do the insurgents want? Political pluralism and parliamentary democracy on the Western model, perhaps? Ridiculous even to think of it. Their goal, which many of them do not hide, is to return Afghanistan to feudal and pre-feudal times, to return the land to the landlords, to tear the books from the hands of the peasant, to put the women back in chains.

That is what the Americans are fighting for, under the guise of 'liberation'. That is why we cannot allow them to succeed.

The Afghanistan issue has been systematically and cynically exploited by the USA as a means of pursuing the cold war against the Soviet Union. Far from being the cause of the breakdown of *détente* between East and West, Afghanistan was the result of that breakdown. The US Embassy in Kabul had a solid understanding many months before 1980 of Russian security concerns and of our commitment to establish a more stable regime. The outcry raised by the USA at that time was a propaganda exercise designed to introduce a new cold war.

Our accuser then turns to the Third World conflict and our alleged 'interventions', claiming that Angola is typical. Angola is indeed typical. It is typical both of the power of the people's anti-colonial movements in the Third World, and of the Soviet Union's strict compliance with international law in its relationship with these movements.

The crisis in and around Angola flared up in 1975. The major political force in that country was, just as it is now, the Popular Movement for the Liberation of Angola (MPLA). It had been engaged in a war for liberation from Portuguese rule since the early 1960s. The UN General Assembly supported that struggle by adopting a series of resolutions and urging all nations to render assistance to liberation movements against colonialism in every way. The MPLA sought help from the USA but got a cold shoulder. So they turned to the Soviet Union, and we gave them considerable material aid, to say nothing of moral and political support. All that was strictly in accordance with the UN mandate. As matter of fact, other countries were also helping the MPLA, Sweden among them. In 1974 a revolution took place in Portugal. The new Lisbon government declared its intention to withdraw from all its colonies, including Angola. The MPLA was recognised by most Angolans and by Portugal as the leading political force of the emerging nation.

In spite of this steady advance from the shadows of colonialism, the USA, South Africa and other reactionary powers persisted in intervening in Angolan affairs. They gave support to two rival movements — FNLA and UNITA. The CIA pumped money and arms into these two political factions, which even in colonial times had devoted almost all their energies to fighting the MPLA rather than the Portuguese colonial rulers. South Africa even invaded the Angolan territory, at one point almost reaching the nation's capital.

Faced with foreign aggression, the Angolan government, formed by the MPLA, asked the USSR, Cuba and a number of African nations for help. That help was given. Cuba even sent some military personnel there. Contrary to Western predictions, however, Angola has not been turned into a Soviet colony or military base. Most of the Angolan oil is in fact still extracted by the Gulf Oil Company of Pittsburgh, Pennsylvania. In spite of this, the Cubans are ready to withdraw their personnel step by step, and they even reached an agreement with the Angolan government to do so. But each time the withdrawal had to be postponed in the face of attacks by South African troops and their proxies within Angola. If this danger of aggression is removed, the Cuban personnel would immediately leave.

In summary, the US charge of 'interventionism' against the Soviet Union is a notorious case of 'projection' — imputing to others its own evil designs. Of course the forces of liberation are gaining power everywhere — but the USA cannot face up to the reality that this is because of the power of the people. The only objective scientific studies of intervention carried out in the West in recent years (for instance by the University of Lancaster in Britain), showed that the USA 'intervened' militarily in foreign conflicts at least ten times as much as the Soviet Union between 1945 and 1980! Let us now turn to this grim record.

US Expansionism since World War II — Prosecution

Accused: The USA.

Case for the Prosecution:

The end of World War II was the beginning of a thrust towards a world capitalist empire by the USA. Massive military alliances were constructed to 'contain' the Soviet Union, and a pattern of intervention in Third World conflicts was established to crush by military force or intrigue any social movement hostile to capitalism.

The final phase of American imperialism began with the dropping of the first atomic bomb on Hiroshima in 1945 — an action clearly calculated as much as a warning to Russia as a superfluous measure for terminating the war with Japan. This act symbolised the transformation of America from a country which once boasted of its immunity from 'Old World militarism' into the most heavily armed nation the world has ever seen. For the first time a large conscript army was kept up in peacetime, as well as a formidable navy and air force, all drawn together under the National Security Act of 1947 into a unified so-called 'Defense System'. Leading figures from the armed forces now became prominent in the power élite, and the 'Pentagon', the US Department of Defense, grew into that vast city of military bureaucracy which still dominates US foreign policy. This was the direct outcome of the Great Patriotic War which left on the one hand a devastated Europe, with its empires collapsing, and on the other hand, the USA vastly enriched, and in sole possession of the 'weapon to end all other weapons' — the atomic bomb. The temptation to make a bid for world empire was irresistible.

The Cold War in its overt form, however, began with an internal conflict in Greece. The conflict was not with Moscow, since it had been agreed that Greece was in the Western sphere of influence. A civil war erupted soon after the war between a right wing fascist group and a socialist movement. Britain intervened on the side of the right wing, in spite of the fact that it included many former Nazi sympathisers; and Britain brought in the USA. Anti-communist hysteria was whipped up in Britain and America, exploiting the Greek situation to create an anti-Soviet front. Truman proclaimed the doctrine of 'supporting free people everywhere', and the Marshall Plan was introduced to pour American capital into Western Europe and so consolidate the dollar empire. Meanwhile, in China, another civil war was going on between Chiang Kai-shek and a people's revolution. Chiang Kai-shek's government was corrupt, incompetent and totally lacking in popular support. The British Foreign Office China expert, Sir John Platt, said that propping it up was like trying to pin apple jelly on to a wall. But the British and Americans supported it because it was anti-communist. When the inevitable defeat followed, this provided even more fuel for the anti-communist mania, and helped to fuel 'McCarthyism' in the USA — the systematic persecution of anyone who has remote alleged connections either with socialism or with Russia.

All this, of course, greatly helped to tie Western Europe to the USA as a new extension of the US dollar empire and a bulwark of capitalism. A network of military alliances was formed which had nothing in common other than their hatred of Russia. NATO was formed to include Greece and Turkey, countries without a vestige of democracy. The USA was quite happy to have Franco's fascist Spain in as well as a member of their 'free world' although the Europeans could not quite swallow this pill. The purpose of NATO was not and is not to preserve 'freedom' but to preserve US supremacy.

From 1948, when the USA deployed strategic bombers in Britain and then decided to maintain a military presence in West Germany, NATO has served to perpetuate the US military occupation of Western Europe. So flagrant were the US intentions that Charles de Gaulle withdrew France from the military wing of NATO in 1967, declaring flatly that France was not willing to become 'America's Algeria'.

The USA has maintained hegemony primarily through a monopoly control over the NATO nuclear stockpile and the presence of 250,000 US troops in Europe, as well as by its massive technical assistance to individual NATO countries' military machines. Exercising this control has not been easy or without its tensions. When the USA first proposed in 1954 that US 'tactical' nuclear weapons be deployed in Europe, the NATO members were reluctant. Acquiescence was obtained by whipping up the 'Soviet threat' to the necessary level of hysteria. NATO has always been reluctant to accept the American strategic doctrine as well. In 1967, when the doctrine of so-called 'flexible response' was adopted (which commits the USA to first-use of nuclear weapons), the NATO members demanded that they be given greater influence over the use of the weapons deployed on their soil. The only concession the USA would make was to permit the establishment of the NATO Nuclear Planning Group, which would allow for joint consultations on targeting of the weapons. The USA retained exclusive control and possession of the warheads themselves. In the case of the Cruise and Pershing II missiles, while Britain, West Germany, Holland, Belgium and Italy have some say on where they might be deployed, the missiles themselves will remain under US control. They can be released only on US authority.

US control over the nuclear weapons stockpile gives it leadership in

NATO. Thus NATO unity is based on the supremacy of its superpower. This unity is made tolerable because of the political indoctrination that accompanies the US military presence. The 'Soviet threat' is constantly used to justify, continue and increase US domination. West Germany is the most firmly controlled NATO member, perhaps because it is closest to the 'Russian threat'. The US domination of Britain, however, is also pervasive and so deeply entrenched as to have become part of the British way of life. It is commonly referred to as 'the special relationship'.

Western Europe is, of course, the main bastion of American power against the Soviet Union. But the fight against the forces of nationalism and liberation has to be waged on a world-wide basis. The USA accuses the Soviet Union of military 'interventionism'; yet by far the most notorious intervention of recent history was the American war in Vietnam, which lasted for ten years and cost millions of lives. This war was an attempt by the USA to stem the tide of a national liberation movement by propping up a corrupt and decadent regime.

As you know, before the Great Patriotic War Vietnam was a French colony. The Americans assisted the French in their fight to keep control of the colony, but the French were nevertheless resoundingly defeated at Dien Bien Phu in 1954. In the peace treaty which followed (the 'Geneva Accords'), it was aggreed that the country should be temporarily divided into north and south regions, but that national elections under international superpowers should be held in 1956 to unify the country. A popular communist regime was established in the north, and a US puppet dictatorship in the south. The southern dictator, Ngo Dinh Diem, refused to have elections because he said the Communist would cheat. In fact he refused because he knew the Communists would win; and the Americans, who also knew this from their own intelligence sources, backed him up. As opposition to the dictator Diem grew, so the USA increased the number of their so-called military 'advisers' in the south from 900 to 16,000 — imagine 16,000 advisers! Eventually even the Americans realised that Diem was a liability and they organised his removal in favour of a group of generals, who subsequently murdered him. It was too late, however, to stem the tide of liberation. A people's movement determined to throw off colonialism was gathering strength. There was no question of the 'north' invading the 'south'. This was one country, illegally divided because elections had been blocked, and the Vietnamese were fighting for their country and their freedom.

The Americans looked for an excuse to wage war on the north and bomb it into submission. On 4 August 1964 President Johnson said that two US destroyers had been attacked by the North Vietnamese in the Gulf of Tonkin, off the coast of Vietnam. This was a lie, as we now know from the testimony of the US airforce pilot who was supposed to have reported the attack. Yet it provided the excuse the Americans needed to step up the war until over *half a million* US troops were fighting in Vietnam, armed with all the most modern and horrific weaponry of the world's military superpower — helicopters, napalm, agent orange, flamethrowers, saturation bombing. They bombed and bombed again, killing over a million Vietnamese in their own country. Yet such was the courage of the people determined to resist the hated colonial power that the Americans eventually had to acknowledge defeat and withdraw. They left behind a pathetic puppet regime in the south, which lasted only months, until Vietnam was united once more.

No Russian or Chinese troops took part in this war. It was an American war — of military imperialism which failed because of the power of the people.

As regards Latin America, the consistent policy of the USA since 1945 has been 'dictatorship by proxy' — dictatorship both of an economic and a military kind. As a distinguished US historian put it, in Central America all governments are acceptable — provided they are anti-communist; and all (even the outrageously tyrannical and corrupt regime of former President Duvalier in Haiti) receive aid to bolster their armed forces and their economies. Hereditary dictatorships are seen as 'stabilising forces'.

If, however, things went wrong with empire by proxy, intervention was never far behind. In 1965, in the Dominican Republic, the long and brutal despotism of Trujillo was rounded off by his murder. A period of chaos followed in which it was clearly possible that a genuine people's government might be established. The House of Representatives in the USA carried a resolution that 'The US or any other American country has a right of intervention in order to keep communism outside the Western Hemisphere'. US troops were accordingly despatched, and the result was the consolidation in power of Dr Balaguer, whose ruthless and repressive regime became a legend throughout Latin America.

In Chile another technique was used. In 1970 a politician sympathetic to Marxism was constitutionally elected to power to head a broad front of democratic parties. In order to defend their interests, the USA, acting largely through the CIA, organised and triggered off a counter-revolution — beginning with a process of economic strangulation, and ending with a bloodthirsty army coup in 1973, resulting in a sustained reign of terror quite new in Chilean history, under a regime whose evil influence persists to this day.

Finally, the most notorious recent display of American military imperialism is there for all the world to see in Reagan's attempt to destroy the democratic government of Nicaragua. For a country whose constitution is founded on human rights, and which prides itself on observation of international law, the story of US relations with Nicaragua is the greatest scandal of our day — and most of America's allies know it.

It is worth recalling a bit of history here. Central America is a region of immense social degradation and poverty, side by side with American big business interests. It is indeed America's yard — America's slave economy moved further south. Nicaragua is one of the poorest countries in the region. For over thirty years, until 1979, the notorious Somoza family, with US support, ran Nicaragua like a personal feudal estate, controlled by the so-called 'national guard' — the Somozas' personal thug army. By 1979 it was estimated that Anastasio Somoza (the younger son of the first Somoza) personally owned assets to the value of over $500 million. One firm came to symbolise Somoza's business interests — Plasmaferesis, a company jointly owned with anti-Castro Cubans which bought blood from poor Nicaraguans for sale in the USA.

In the 1970s the brutality and corruption of the Somozas also alienated business leaders and the traditional opposition parties. These middle class groups brought economic resources and international respectability to the anti-Somoza movement. A guerrilla army of 'Sandinista' freedom-fighters was formed, naming themselves after the national hero Sandino, who fought against a previous US invasion way back in 1913, and rebelled against the corrupt government. After six weeks of fighting, the national guard collapsed, and Somoza fled to the USA taking with him most of the country's wealth.

The new government, which included a number of distinguished members of the Roman Catholic Society of Jesus (the Jesuits), was passionately dedicated to human rights and human development.

In the literacy crusade organised by the liberation movement, literacy rose from 50 per cent to 85 per cent, health expenditure increased dramatically, infant mortality fell from 127 per 1000 to 87 per 1000. Somoza's assets were confiscated and the banks were nationalised. The Sandinistas were clearly dedicated to distributing wealth and raising the standards of the people.

In spite of this the US government has waged a hate campaign against the new regime from the outset, and President Reagan made it quite clear that his objective was to destroy the new government by military, economic and diplomatic means. Nicaragua today is under constant attack from armed opponents of its revolution (the 'contras') based in neighbouring countries and supported by the USA. Revelations of US support for 'covert' operations against Nicaragua, including the mining of ports, have provoked outrage in the US Congress and condemnation from the International Court of Justice. The US government neglects no opportunity to denounce Nicaragua as a threat to Central America as a whole, and reinforces this propaganda campaign with economic and diplomatic pressure designed to weaken the Nicaraguan economy and create internal tension.

We noted with interest that the USA did not select Nicaragua to substantiate its charge of 'military expansionism' against the Soviet Union — although the only justification to the world for their behaviour in Nicaragua has to be the 'Soviet threat'. Is it not strange that Nicaragua's 150 tanks can pose a security threat to the USA which has 15,000 tanks, 75 times the population and 100 times the GNP? Is it even likely that they pose a security threat to El Salvador or Guatemala which are unapproachable by tanks from Nicaragua except by a very long hazardous haul along the inter-American highway? It is obvious to a military mind that neither the jagged mountains of the north nor the swampy forested lowlands of the Atlantic Coast are passable for modern 36-ton battle tanks. Clearly these tanks are for use *within* Nicaragua — not elsewhere; for use, therefore, only against an invading force.

Why indeed are so many men under arms in Nicaragua, except in response to intimidation by the world's greatest military power — namely the USA? And if the Nicaraguan government is governing against the will of the people, how come they can raise and equip such a large people's militia?

In November 1984 free elections were held in Nicaragua in the presence of many international observers and were widely reported to be free and fair. These elections confirmed a massive Sandinist majority. Yet still the US President persists in his attempts to undermine the Nicaraguan government, continues to train and aid the rebels and mercenary armies, and appears poised to invade — an option which the President refuses to renounce.

If military imperialism is in full spate anywhere in the world today, it is so in Central America. It is this fact which makes America's European allies increasingly restive as they find themselves bound to a policy which denies those very freedoms on which their alliance was supposed to be founded.

US Expansionism since World War II — Defence

Accused: The USA.

Case for the Defence:

Far from being out to dominate the world, the USA is the only state in history to have had world empire offered on a plate, and to have rejected it, preferring to be part of a world-wide association of free peoples.

If, as it is alleged, the USA had a dream of 'world empire', and expansion without limit at the end of World War II, then it is somewhat odd that we began this process by a massive withdrawal of US forces from Europe. It is well known that US forces in Europe were only built up again as it became clear that the Communist forces in Eastern Europe were there to stay, whatever the will of the people. The blockade of Berlin by the Russians in 1948 confirmed that the Soviet Union would make use of its vast military superiority to force an unwilling people into the Eastern camp. What should the USA have done? Confronted by massive forces trained, equipped and prepared for invasion of the West, should the USA have simply abandoned its friends and allies? To have done so would have been to abandon everything one fought for. NATO was formed in response to this threat.

It is worth recalling that at the end of World War II, the USA was overwhelmingly the most powerful economic power in the world, and was the sole possessor of nuclear weapons. Had she wished to do so, she could undoubtedly have established a world empire, a 'Pax Americana' for which there could have been strong moral justification. This was a unique point in history, when world empire was possible *and was refused*. The moral significance of this should never be forgotten.

As for Marshall Aid, the money poured into devastated Europe at the end of World War II — that so-called instrument of colonialism — the plan was directed, as Marshall himself declared, 'not against any country or doctrine, but against hunger, poverty, desperation and chaos'. It was also, of course, as Marshall went on to say, designed to foster 'the political and social conditions on which free institutions can exist'. This is a strange kind of colonialism! Out of this act of generosity a free association of people developed in the form of the Atlantic alliance. Within this alliance, as our accuser is very well aware, each country is perfectly free to make its own decisions — to accept or not accept weapons, free indeed to get out of the alliance altogether. They know that no US tanks will roll in their capital cities if they do so.

US nuclear forces in Europe, far from being a symbol of domination, are there at the urgent demand of all European powers, simply to guarantee them against the threat from the East. This is nothing other than a contract between free people.

As for Vietnam, it is a scandalous misrepresentation of history to accuse the USA of being heirs to French colonialism. The USA was a leading opponent of French colonial rule, as of all colonial rule, and was only drawn into Vietnam because the northern dictator, Ho Chi Minh, threatened to impose a rigid Marxist dictatorship not only over Vietnam but over the whole of South East Asia. Ngo Dinh Diem, the South Vietnamese president whom the USA supported, was himself an ardent Vietnamese patriot and had a deep hatred of colonial rule. It is true that the USA made mistakes, but they were mainly the mistake of thinking too highly of our friends. It turned out that the regime we supported did not command allegiance of the people.

Our reasons for being in Vietnam, however, were none other than to preserve the right of the Vietnamese people to freedom and self-determination. We had no commercial interest in Vietnam; we certainly had no intention of establishing any colonial rule — the American people would never entertain such an idea. We were there to fight for human rights.

As for the US record in Latin America, it is well established that Cuba has an extensive programme dedicated to the export of revolution throughout the Western hemisphere. This takes the form of training guerrilla armies from other countries, supply of weapons and ammunition, espionage, propaganda and policies of political destabilisation. In all this activity Cuba is backed by the Soviet Union. If the USA did not combat this activity, the entire region would soon fall into the hands of Marxist dictatorships and freedom would be lost forever.

Of course some of the regimes which are opposed to Communism are not ideal Western democracies, but with our help they can move towards genuine freedom in a way that would be barred if the Communists took over. El Salvador and Guatemala also are already making dramatic progress in this direction.

Our objective in Central America was clearly set out in a report to the President of the USA by the Secretary of State in 1985. It is to promote strong economies, with fairer distribution of wealth, and democratic and free societies.

Military imperialism is hardly the term to apply to this historic mission which the USA has to carry out as a trustee for humanity.

Superpower Military Confrontation since 1945 — the Western Case

The Soviet Union has since the end of World War II pursued a consistent policy of building up its military power to ensure overall military superiority over the West. With the 'correlation of forces' in its favour, it will be able successfully to pursue its single minded objective of world Communism. The US military preparations have had the sole purpose of containing the spread of Soviet power.

The hard military facts about the Soviet Union since 1945 totally belie its peace propaganda, which is simply a cloak for its policy of military domination and expansion.

As regards conventional or non-nuclear forces, we have already pointed out that it was the Soviet refusal to demobilise and continued military domination of Europe which triggered off the defence reaction of the Western powers. Without going into the details of what happened between then and now, we simply have to review the present 'correlation of forces' in Central Europe to realise that what has happened is the systematic, consistent and effective build-up of Soviet forces ready and able to attack the West.

No one has the slightest doubt that Soviet forces in Central Europe vastly outnumber those of the NATO alliance. This is true in practically all categories of weapons — but it is particularly true of tanks, which outnumber those of NATO by 3 to 1. The tanks are important because they are the centrepiece of Soviet plans for a 'blitzkrieg' attack into Western Europe, a lightning attack with massed tanks, infantry and aircraft. Make no mistake about it, this *is* what Soviet military planning is all about. Anyone can verify it by checking with military experts — *whether from the West or from the East*. The Western posture, on the other hand, is and always has been purely for defence — to 'restore and maintain' the integrity of Western Europe, in the words of the NATO treaty. We have no plans or ability to invade Eastern Europe or Russia, and they know it.

A development in the 1970s which has been particularly threatening to NATO has been a threefold increase in Soviet fighter bombers and helicopters, which can both support a blitzkrieg on the ground and simultaneously strike deep into our territory and destroy our supply lines and bases.

On the nuclear front, there is exactly the same long-term tendency to overwhelming superiority on the Soviet side. The most dramatic development in recent years has been the threefold increase in the 1970s of land-based intercontinental missiles — especially the notorious SS18s. The significance of these is that they can destroy American missiles or other military targets *before we have a chance to use them* — they are part of what are called in military jargon 'time-urgent, hard-target kill capability'. The big intercontinental missiles now deployed by the Soviet Union have highly accurate 'multiple reentry vehicles' (MIRVs). That means each missile carries a whole cluster of nuclear weapons, which together can knock out most important military installations in the USA. No one denies that the Soviet Union has a tremendous advantage over the USA in this respect. They could eliminate a large proportion of our ICBMs at one blow in a pre-emptive strike. The correlation of forces has certainly shifted towards the East in big nuclear weapons as well as in conventional ones.

All this developed in the 1970s — the period of so-called *détente*. It's hard to believe that the Soviet Union got into this position of superiority by accident. Why should they put so much effort into getting into a position to destroy most of our nuclear weapons, when we are not in a position to destroy theirs? Far from being content with 'parity', and loyal to the spirit of the 1972 SALT I agreement, the Soviet Union continued without any respite throughout the 1970s with the build-up of their nuclear forces. Brezhnev even told Nixon in May 1972 that the Soviet Union had every intention of pushing ahead with programmes in areas not covered by the agreement. Worse than that, they cheated by developing a new heavy missile with six warheads, the SS19, contrary to both the letter and spirit of the SALT agreement. This was the very kind of missile most threatening to the USA, since it could clearly destroy American missiles in a first strike.

It's obvious that the Soviet Union wants to be in a position to win a nuclear war — and all their military doctrine makes this quite clear. This should be the final and logical step in the struggle for world domination — the final expansion of the Russian empire. They would not, of course, have to use the weapons; the threat would be enough. They would hold the nuclear ace, and would be able to dominate the USA, and therefore the world. This is what we have to stand up against.

It was also in the 1970s — the period of so-called *détente* — that the Russians began to deploy a new generation of shorter-range nuclear weapons for use in Europe — the SS20s, stationed on the Western part of the Soviet Union. These weapons were vastly superior to the SS4s and SS5s which they were supposed to be replacing. They had a range of over 3000 miles and they had three warheads instead of one. They were also mobile and therefore difficult to attack, and they were very much more accurate. The deployment programme of the new weapons proceeded without interruption from mid 1976 right through the SALT II negotiations, without any attempt to discuss or negotiate. Obviously these weapons brought the whole of Europe under much greater threat than before — and they were certainly not a response to any NATO nuclear build-up in Europe, because there wasn't one.

Nor are the SS20s to be considered in isolation. The Soviet Union now has a whole family of missiles (SS21s, 22s, 23s, 24s) all able to attack Western Europe and eliminate virtually all our major military installations at a single stroke.

What then are these weapons for? We don't really have to look for an answer. They are simply a continuation of the consistent Soviet policy of bringing Western Europe into its sphere of influence, and detaching it from the USA.

Having neutralised the Americans' strategic nuclear weapons by achieving 'parity' and removing as they thought the US nuclear guarantee of Europe, the next step forward is to overshadow Europe with a selective nuclear threat, which will bring Europe completely under their influence. The SS20s and their cousins are the ideal weapons for that purpose.

To complete the picture, there is the question of Soviet Star Wars. In 1972 the Soviet Union and the USA agreed not to develop extensive *defences* against ballistic missiles — on the grounds that we were each vulnerable to the other's, and this meant that there was a sort of mutual hostage arrangement called 'MAD' (Mutual Assured Destruction). Accordingly, the USA built up no defences in the 1970s — we have virtually no air defence over the USA, no defence against missiles, no defence against nuclear weapons. However, the Soviet Union never accepted the mutual hostage idea. They welcomed the ABM treaty as a way of keeping the USA vulnerable, but under its cover they poured enormous resources into development of an anti-missile system for the USSR. They have a deployed system round Moscow which is being rapidly upgraded and could quickly be expanded nationwide; and they have the most advanced air defence system in the world (at least twenty times as great as that of the USA) which could readily be upgraded into an anti-missile defence.

Such a development, if not counteracted, would finally set the seal on Soviet worldwide military superiority. Behind a defence shield her vastly superior nuclear forces would dominate the world. This is the end towards which Russian military policy, backed by Marxist theory, is inevitably directed. The task of the USA is to preserve freedom and democracy throughout the world in the face of this threat. As the most powerful nation in the free world, it is our responsibility to stand firm against this threat, and thus to ensure peace with freedom for all peoples.

Superpower Military Confrontation since 1945 — the Eastern Case

The Soviet Union has found itself under perpetual threat from the USA since 1945, and has reacted by taking appropriate defence measures. Its objective is equality of military power to counterbalance the Western threat. Unlike the USA, it does not seek superiority, nor does it seek to extend its power by military force.

Since our opponent refers again to the beginning of the Cold War, it is worth noting that recently declassified document in the West are throwing a very different light on this matter from that which has been peddled up to now by Western propaganda.

We must remember the deep-rooted hostility of the USA and Britain to the Soviet regime, which goes right back to the wars of intervention in 1918. This hostility was concealed, but not changed, by the wartime alliance against Germany. *Immediately* after the war ended, the mood in the West changed. The dropping of the atom bomb on Hiroshima was in large part, as US Secretary of War Stimson recorded in his diary, 'to persuade Russia to play ball'. Massive economic aid was poured into Western Europe, but was offered in a way carefully calculated to be rejected by Russia. The notorious Iron Curtain speech of Churchill in 1946 was agreed with Truman, the new Cold War president of the USA, and was a virtual declaration of war. Its purpose was to eradicate the feelings of good will towards Russia which had grown up among the people.

Meanwhile, in the military field, plans for using atomic weapons against the Soviet Union were immediately put in train. *By the end of 1945* the US Joint Chiefs of Staff were talking about eliminating twenty of our largest cities in a first strike with 196 atom bombs. The evidence is there for everyone to read in documents such as Report 329 of the Joint Intelligence Committee of the US Joint Chiefs of Staff (December

1945). Between 1946 and 1949 a whole series of war plans were developed, culminating in 'Dropshot' — a plan for using 300 atom bombs against the Soviet Union ('atomising' was the current term), and even elaborating rules of conduct for the subsequent occupation of our territory. Our intelligence services are not so inefficient that we did not have some warning of these plans. We did not even need our intelligence services, however, to see that we were being ringed by hostile military alliances. This process began in 1947, and continued throughout the 1950s. The list of anti-Soviet alliances speaks for itself: the Western Hemisphere Defence Treaty Organisation in 1947, establishing US alliances throughout North and South America; the North Atlantic Treaty Organisation (NATO) in 1949, allying the USA with twelve nations of Western Europe; the Australia–New Zealand–United States Treaty (ANZUS) in 1951; the South-East Asia Treaty Organisation (SEATO) in 1954, bringing together the Philippines, Thailand, Pakistan, Australia and New Zealand with Britain and France; and the Central Treaty Organisation in the Middle East (CENTO) in 1959, linking Turkey, Iraq, Iran, Pakistan and Britain. In a little more than a decade after World War II in which the USA and USSR had fought as allies, the USA surrounded the USSR with 400 major as well as 2000 auxiliary bases spread around the world.

How was the Soviet Union to respond? How were we to maintain our rights of self-defence and self-determination guaranteed under the UN Charter? What would *any* great power do when faced with such a conspiracy? I submit that they would do precisely what we did. Maintain military readiness to thwart aggression. That is why we maintained and continue to maintain forces in Europe to preserve our territorial integrity.

As for nuclear weapons, it is hardly to be wondered at that in response to the US policy of dominating the Soviet Union by nuclear threats, the Soviet Union developed its own atom bombs; and this has been the story of the arms race ever since. The driving force throughout has been the USA.

In August 1945 the world learned of the appearance of the most destructive weapon in history — the atomic bomb. Not only did the USA develop the bomb, it actually used it, and with no military need. The result was that 273,000 people in Hiroshima and Nagasaki were killed and 195,000 received fatal doses of radiation. Subsequent Soviet proposals for banning the use of nuclear energy for military purposes were turned down by the USA. So, in face of this grave threat, the Soviet Union took countermeasures and developed its own atomic weaponry.

The same is true of all subsequent developments. The USA became the initiator of a strategic armaments race. In the 1950s, on the pretext of having 'fallen behind in bombers', the Pentagon obtained large allocations from Congress and set in motion a crash programme for the construction of strategic bombers. After an armada of these aircraft had been built, however, it was 'discovered' that the Americans had deliberately exaggerated the number of Soviet bombers three to four times over. In the early 1960s a cry was raised about a 'US missile gap', and the USA initiated a massive deployment of land-based intercontinental ballistic missiles (ICBMs). Then, after more than a thousand of these had been deployed, it turned out that the Soviet 'missile threat' had been exaggerated fifteen to twenty times over.

Simultaneously, an American programme was launched to build forty-one nuclear-powered ballistic missile submarines (SSBNs). At that time, no one in the world had them. At the end of the 1960s and the beginning of the 1970s, the USA was the first to begin arming strategic ballistic missiles with highly accurate multiple independently targetable re-entry vehicles (MIRVs), thus sharply increasing the total of nuclear warheads. When the Soviet Union followed suit, we again had the cry of Soviet superiority raised in the Pentagon, preparing the way for yet another escalation in the form of Star Wars.

The idea that the Americans simply sat back in the 1970s and waited for the Soviet Union to catch up in the arms race is patently false. Its purpose is obviously to justify the Western build-up in the 1980s, by frightening people into thinking they are being 'overtaken' in some deadly duel. In fact what happened was a huge American build-up of *warheads* — that is the actual nuclear bombs, the things that do the damage. They pushed ahead as rapidly as they possibly could in the 1970s with the 'MIRVing' of their missiles. As a result of this in the so-called sleeping seventies, the number of long-range US warheads on land able to attack independent targets increased from 1000 to 2000 — and in the sea from 650 to 5000. Quite apart from this, the sleeping seventies saw the beginning of work on a whole new generation of weapons which came to the surface in the 1980s — the new Trident submarine, the B1 bomber, the Cruise missile.

SS20s

The idea that Soviet SS20s present a new threat to Europe is another patent example of the way the Americans have always built up a fear of the Soviet Union to achieve their own military ends.

The facts are that the Soviet SS20s are replacements for old-fashioned missiles which were deployed twenty years ago (the SS4s and SS5s), and which have become obsolete. These replacements had been planned and foreseen for at least ten years. The purpose of the new weapons is just the same as that of the old ones — to deter and counterbalance the American nuclear weapons based in Europe and aimed against Russia and the Warsaw Pact. These American forward-based systems number about 1600 delivery systems, together with US submarines carrying long-range missiles, nuclear armed planes or aircraft carriers in the Mediterranean and the North Atlantic, as well as the numerous missiles and planes of America's nuclear allies in Europe, Britain and France.

The important point is that the SS20s cannot reach the USA and do not threaten the USA. The new American systems in Europe, however, do threaten Russia very directly — and that is obviously their purpose. Europe has been turned into a massive American aircraft and missile carrier on the very borders of the Soviet Union. The Pershing IIs can reach Moscow in ten minutes from West Germany, and destroy the centre of our political life — 'decapitate the enemy', in the jargon of the US nuclear war-fighters. We know that at the same time the Pentagon was planning to fill Europe with Cruise missiles aimed at our western front, she was also considering how to locate cruise missiles in Korea to threaten us in the east. To complete the picture, remember also that the USA planned to deploy 5000 Cruise missiles on aircraft and many more thousands at sea. If you add to this picture the clear purpose of the USA, expressed by Weinberger, which was to achieve total nuclear superiority over the Soviet Union as in the 1950s, then the whole European deployment of new American missiles falls clearly into place. Of course the Americans pretended that the pressure came from the

Europeans, and as usual they were expert at manipulating European fears; but as one eminent US General put it, 'If you believe that the Europeans persuaded the Americans to deploy these missiles in Europe, you must believe in Father Christmas'.

The nuclear blackmail argument which the Americans use against the Soviet Union is yet another blatant example of what the psychologists call 'projection' — blaming the other person for what you are doing yourself. The whole purpose of ringing the Soviet Union with forward-based missiles is obviously intimidation of the Soviet Union — and it is quite clear that the USA thinks in this way, and has always done so. There is, however, nothing in Soviet military doctrine which suggests for a moment that SS20s can be used to intimidate Europe. The idea that we might tell the French we would bomb Paris unless they made some concession is pure nonsense — political nonsense and military nonsense as well. But it is a kind of nonsense which fits American doctrine, and reveals as in a mirror their own true purposes.

The US argument that its missiles are vulnerable to a Soviet first strike is another example of fear propaganda, designed to justify the US offensive build-up. It is true that we followed the American lead in developing weapons which can strike enemy missiles, and both sides are now in a position to do this — that is to destroy some of each other's missiles. The American say we can destroy nearly all of theirs, and they can only destroy half of ours; but they only reach this conclusion by talking about missiles on the land, and forgetting those in the air and at sea. The fact is that we have a mainly land-based force — 70 per cent of our warheads are on land, and 24 per cent of the Americans'. It's hardly surprising then that our 70 per cent can have a drastic effect on their 24 per cent — but what about all those *other* weapons the USA has at sea and in the air? The USA is always talking about its strategic 'triad'. Even if they believed for a moment that the Soviet Union would be mad enough to make a first strike against the US land-based weapons — and even if we were *totally* successful — then the USA would still have 3000 weapons at sea and in the air, at least six times as many as would be needed to destroy every major city in the USSR! Why then do they need more? Obviously because they themselves want to be able to strike first and win. What they accuse us of is what they seek themselves. They use the Soviet Union as a mirror in which their own diabolic image appears.

The final nonsense of our opponents' case is to blame Star Wars on the Soviet Union. Everyone knows that Star Wars is President Reagan's own personal initiative. Of course the Soviet Union has a massive air defence against the threat of mass bomb attack from the West. We also have an anti-missile defence round our capital city — exactly as was agreed in the ABM treaty, to which we have always adhered. The USA makes a fuss about our alleged technical violations of the ABM treaty — by building a phased-array space tracking radar at Krasnoyarsk, for instance — but they prefer to shout about this in public rather than discuss it in the Standing Consultative Commission set up by the treaty precisely to deal with this kind of allegation. In fact the US government must know that an official classified report to the British Cabinet expresses the view that the Krasnoyarsk radar is *not* a violation of the ABM treaty, and that opinion about alleged Soviet violations is sharply divided even within the US Administration.

The USA continues to play its old game of exaggerating the 'Soviet threat' to justify their own offensive build-up — and incidentally to destroy the ABM treaty that is one of the main achievements of twenty years of arms control.

The USSR does not seek and has never sought military superiority.

Of course we believe that the balance of forces in the world is tending inevitably in favour of those who work for national liberation, and for the liberation of people from economic oppression. These forces are evidently gaining steadily over the forces of capitalist imperialism and domination. All these forces of liberation ultimately favour socialism, because socialism is their natural conclusion. Of course we rejoice in this great forward march of history and we are privileged to take part in it.

That does not mean, however, that we seek or have ever sought military superiority. When we talk about the 'correlation of forces' which is changing in our favour, we think particularly of social forces, the forces of the people. There is now a rough parity in armed forces between the Soviet Union and the USA, and this is what we desire.

We do not seek military superiority, but neither will we allow the forces of capitalism to win superiority over us. The military equilibrium objectively serves to safeguard world peace; it is the quest for superiority which destroys it.

RW-D

Provided parity can be preserved, our objective in military terms must be to remove for ever the threat of nuclear weapons from mankind. Our leader has now proposed a bold and imaginative plan to eliminate all nuclear weapons by the end of the century. This is surely an objective desired by all peoples, and it is in the name of all peoples that we speak.

Verdict

We the jury, speaking in the name of *Homo sapiens* resident on the planet of earth, have been held in thrall by the debate between these opposing parties. We do not intend to pronounce judgement upon the contestants.

The history of humankind, like our own personal histories, has many possible meanings. If it were not so, we would have no task to perform, no responsibility to fulfil. It is the future which is continuously resolving the ambiguities of the past, and the future is our responsibility. The ambiguities of the present are the very clay which we need for our potter's wheel. If the clay were already set, our hands would be useless. Our task is to fashion a precious heirloom for future generations. As the wheel of history spins, so we must use our hands to shape the future.

Nowhere is the ambiguity of our history more evident than in perceptions of defence and offence. This ambiguity is very deeply rooted in our human nature and even in our prehuman nature. Anyone who has faced a cornered animal will know how closely related are fear and aggression — defence and offence. Which of us even in our most aggressive and expansionist moods does not have an element of fear lurking in our hearts? Which of us would not claim defence as a justification for our offensive acts?

Of course some states are more aggressive than others. But by what percentage? 90 per cent aggressive, and 10 per cent defensive — or 60 per cent aggressive, and 40 per cent defensive? Clearly there can be no answer — not through lack of information, but because meanings are indeterminate, incomplete, and therefore 'open' to future resolution. One thing is quite certain, and that is the perceptions of opponents will never coincide.

The potter's wheel

Instead, therefore, of seeking to determine what is of its very nature indeterminate, we choose instead to draw attention to significant similarities in the manner in which the opponents conduct their defence.

First, with regard to the charge of military expansionism there is a remarkable coincidence between the language of the two accused. Both appear to be passionately dedicated to the principle of self-determination of peoples — to the right of any people to determine its own social and political system, without any forcible intervention from outside. It was interesting to note that neither side made any claim whatsoever which would contradict that principle.

The Soviet Union, for instance, did not mention the so-called 'Brezhnev doctrine', announced by the Soviet leader Brezhnev just after the alleged intervention by the Soviet Union in Czechoslovakia. According to that doctrine, when socialism is threatened in one country, this is a matter of concern to all socialist states. This concern seems perfectly reasonable — but the question is, does this concern give one socialist state a right to invade another? The Soviet Union seems to refute this idea. Their alleged intervention, they argue, as in Afghanistan, is always by invitation of a legitimate government, always to help ward off a threat.

The USA accused similarly did not appeal to the much more venerable 'Monroe doctrine', which was proclaimed by President Monroe in 1823, and appeared to give the USA extensive veto powers over the affairs of all states in North, Central and South America. The alleged interventions or threatened interventions, they argue, are all made in accordance with international law — either at the request of a friendly government, or to rescue US citizens from immediate peril. The accused claimed no right to intervene in Nicaragua (although he made it clear he did not much like the Sandinista regime). We note also that aid given by the USA to rebels in Nicaragua is 'covert'. Covert actions are actions which states take 'unofficially', without going through the formal process of law, without proclaiming their actions to the world. They are actions, therefore, which do not have any 'normative' effect — they are *not* meant to establish precedents, they are *not* actions that are proclaimed rightful. Indeed, by taking 'covert' action a state goes a long way towards proclaiming that act illegal.

Hypocrisy

The contestants will no doubt accuse each other of notorious hypocrisy. But this accusation misses the point. Hypocrisy is the tribute paid by vice to virtue. It provides the very material from which the cloth of international law is woven. He who proclaims a just law and breaks it fashions a halter for his own neck. The Western powers in World Wars I and II married themselves to the principle of self-determination, which helped to undermine the European empire of their adversaries. They did not anticipate that, by the force of the same principle, they would soon have to preside over the dissolution of their own empires!

We have indeed heard strong evidence of hypocrisy on either side: the fraudulent Gulf of Tonkin incident, which enabled the USA to justify its attacks on North Vietnam as self-defence, the imaginary invitation from Czechoslovakia and threat of West German infiltration which enabled the Soviet Union to pose as liberators in 1968. Both frauds show the concern of the contestants for the principle of international law.

We further note, with even greater satisfaction, that both of the accused are totally dedicated to the pursuit of human rights. Although they renounce the right to intervene by military force in the internal affairs of other states, or to trespass on each other's 'spheres of influence', they nevertheless express a powerful concern for the rights of all peoples. This is both commendable and normal, since the constitutions both of the Soviet Union and of the USA are founded explicitly on a doctrine of liberation. In this respect they are both heirs to a historical tradition, which dates back to the liberation of the Israelites from slavery in Egypt — a tradition continued through Christianity and through the French Revolution. The American Declaration of Independence, using the same language as that of the earlier revolutionaries, proclaims that all human beings are equal in dignity and rights, and denies the legitimacy of any government which oppresses its people.

Furthermore, both the USA and the USSR are signatories to the International Conventions of Human Rights, which affirm the right of every man, woman and child on the face of the earth to life, education, work, health care, freedom of expression, freedom from political oppression, freedom of self-determination. Not only is it understandable, therefore, that both sides should take an active interest in the rights of oppressed peoples throughout the world, it appears that they are legally obliged to do so.

Of course the two sides emphasise different aspects of human rights. In general, the USA proclaims its support for 'freedom rights' — the right to political freedom — and the Soviet Union stresses 'justice rights' — the right to work, food and shelter. It is clear, however that the two kinds of rights are complementary, and this appears to be the legal position. Food and shelter without freedom is a poor option, but so is freedom without food and shelter.

Finally, we note that both the Soviet Union and NATO make out a very strong case that their military efforts are *entirely defensive* (and that they have no intention whatsoever of imposing their will by force on other people). The Soviet accused has drawn attention to his long and bitter experience of land invasions from the west — an experience that has no parallel in the USA. He has drawn our attention to the West's deeply rooted hostility to the Communist system, regardless of any military threat that system might pose, and to evidence that military action to destroy Communism has been contemplated by the West on a number of occasions. He has drawn our attention to the nuclear threat which the Western powers held over the Soviet Union, refusing to place nuclear competition under genuine international control, and thus generating the arms race from which we now all suffer. Finally, he has drawn our attention to a projected Western military build-up in Central Europe and to aspects of recent US doctrine which suggest that new technology might be used to provide the West with an offensive capability able to destabilise Eastern Europe or strike rapidly and deeply into Warsaw Pact territory, or even decapitate the Soviet Union.

In view of all these facts it is hard to deny that the Soviet Union has both a right and a duty to defend itself against the West by military means.

The Western accused, on the other hand, has argued equally strongly that those military means of so-called 'defence' look suspiciously offensive from the Western side, and that if history gives Russia cause to fear the West, history also gives the West cause to fear the East. It seems hard to deny, in view of the events of Hungary in 1956, in Czechoslovakia in 1968, and more recently in Poland, that these and other East European countries are under the shadow of the Russian military, and have many of the familiar characteristics of a military empire. At the leading edge of this empire, a 1000-km frontier dividing East from West Germany, they have massed military forces greater than anything the world has ever seen in peacetime, and superior in firepower, mobility and readiness to anything the West can line up against them. It may well be, of course, that these forces are there for defensive purposes, as the Soviet maintains. It is very hard to see, however, how the West could ignore the offensive potential. In the face of the Soviet threat, as they perceive it, the West clearly has both a right and a duty to defend itself by military means.

In summary, both sides therefore proclaim the right of self-defence as the sole justification for their military deployments. Both sides utterly reject the charge of military expansionism. Yet it appears that each side has good reason to fear the other. Since there is such a large measure of agreement between the two sides about the principles on which they operate, it seems that it should not be beyond the wit of *Homo sapiens*, for whom we speak, to resolve the military conflict between them. This task seems particularly urgent since the military conflict seems likely to lead to a catastrophe which clearly neither side deserves or intends and which would terminate for ever the tradition of human rights to which they owe their identity.

We strongly urge, therefore, that the two contestants should mount an immediate enquiry into how they might establish systems of defence which, while effectively preserving their own security, do not threaten the security of others; how they might find ways of convincing each other that they mean what they say, and have no aggressive intentions, and how they might progressively dismantle the grotesque military apparatus they have constructed over all our heads, which now threatens to terminate the very existence of humankind in whose name we speak.

2

The Defence of Europe

Coping with Threats

Never in the history of the world has there been such a massive confrontation of military force as that which exists at present in Central Europe. It is there, along a 1000-km frontier, that two huge superpower alliances confront each other eyeball to eyeball, each intent on improving and upgrading its weaponry. The two alliances between them command more than two-thirds of the world's resources, have a dominating influence over nearly half of the world's inhabitants, and control more than half of the world's inhabitable land mass.

Clearly, in terms of world history, we seem to be approaching a kind of 'grand finale'. The final act, however, is not yet written. That is what we are about to do — *we*, the inhabitants of the earth in this very generation.

What is quite clear is that we have to accept the whole reality of war and the threat of war. We are at the culminating point of thousands of years of history. War is part of our heritage, part of our culture and society — part of *us*. Only by accepting it can we control it, only by understanding it can we transcend it. 'Si vis pacem, *para* bellum' was the old military adage — 'if you want peace, prepare for war.' This now needs to be replaced by a new adage — 'If you want peace, understand war', 'Si vis pacem, *stude* bellum.'

What is the West afraid of in Central Europe? Why are our armies there, in military terms? Basically they are there, so the West proclaims and believes, to defend us against a Warsaw Pact attack. When the West looks east, it perceives a very substantial military threat. This perception is not groundless. The East undoubtedly has a great deal

46

more 'invasion equipment' than the West, and appears much more prepared by doctrine and training to use it.

What is feared in the West is something resembling a 'blitzkreig'-type deep and rapid penetration of its territory by hostile forces. Blitzkrieg (which means 'lightning war') is a term which became popular during World War II, and depends heavily on the kind of armoured fighting vehicles which we invented at the end of World War I. To preserve their secrecy in order to achieve maximum impact on enemy morale, they were given the name 'tanks', since the early ones were rather like water tanks on tracks. The purpose of providing these armoured tractors was to provide a vehicle which would enable an advancing force to more forward safely into hostile territory, even over very rough and muddy ground swept by enemy fire. The vehicles would use caterpillar tracks like farm tractors, would carry steel armour to protect those inside from bullets and shell splinters, and would themselves carry forward 'firepower' in the form of machine guns and light artillery.

Hitler and a few enthusiastic German officers had the imagination to see the revolutionary potential of this new implement of offensive warfare, and with its help, and the shock and deep penetration tactics which accompanied it, he was able quite rapidly to roll forward over most of Western Europe and Eastern Europe — a huge slice of the Soviet Union. It is hardly surprising, in the light of this most recent history of war in Europe, that the West looks with a slightly leery eye at the massed and tank-heavy forces of the Soviet Union in Eastern Europe — bearing in mind, of course, that it was these same forces in the aftermath of the war which helped to impose regimes on people who were not always enthusiastic about them.

Far from diminishing in recent years, the apparent threat from the East has increased. In the case of tanks, the Warsaw Pact enjoys a general 3 to 1 superiority over NATO. Control of the air is also crucial for a successful offensive, and the Soviet tactical air power available on the Central Front has recently improved rapidly in both quality and quantity in relation to NATO's forces. There has also been a marked shift in the nature of the Warsaw Pact tactical air power capabilities. In 1968 Soviet tactical air forces were primarily adapted to the defence of their own airspace, but now the emphasis has shifted dramatically towards an offensive capability, with a shift to bigger range and payload aircraft, and to strike helicopters and fighter bombers, which have the capability of providing close air support along the Central Front and 'deep interdiction' against NATO nuclear weapon sites, supply bases and airfields.

It is not just the military *equipment* of the East that the West is worried about, however. It is the doctrine and training that goes with it. All Warsaw Pact exercises *begin* with an attack from the West of course — just as all Western exercises begin with an attack from the East. What is of more concern for the suspiciously minded military, however, is what follows. The whole thrust of Soviet military deployment, strategy and tactics is to achieve deep and rapid penetration of Western territory.

Many peace-minded people think these are scandalous things to say about the 'peace-loving' Soviet Union. However, if you were to tell a Soviet general that you saw in his forces a military threat to the West, and that you believed he could rapidly invade and occupy Western Europe, I imagine he would be rather flattered. He might well be inclined to think we were grossly underestimating our own defensive capabilities. All the same, he would be pleased that you thought he was doing his job well. He might even be inclined to say if he were also politically minded, 'That is what keeps you from sticking your nose into our business. It's kept the peace for forty years; why should we change it now?'

This does not in any way prove that the Soviet Union is not desirous of peace rather than war. On the contrary, there is ample evidence to prove that as far as the people are concerned the Soviet Union provides a striking example of what Professor Michael Howard has called a 'peace culture', which is in marked contrast to the war culture that prevailed for example in Hitler's Germany. This is hardly surprising, since the Russians lost 20 million of their own people largely on their own territory in the last war, and most families have experienced bereavement. They do not want a repeat performance. So far as the leadership of the Soviet Union is concerned, there is very little evidence of military adventurism, or indeed any possible rational basis for such adventurism. The idea that the Soviet Union might actually wish to compound its problems in Eastern Europe by trying to digest Western Europe as well has a whiff of absurdity about it. It is reminiscent of the song about the woman who eventually swallowed a horse to eat the dog (she's dead!). Virtually no-one with any political education really believes this to be the case.

The Russians do not want a war — but if there is one, they want to win it. That's the job of the military. In order to do this job, the Soviet Union has a military posture based on *offensive* defence. Offensive is not an abusive word; it is a technical military term with a well-established meaning. An army incapable of *taking the offensive* when necessary would not be worth its salt, in military tradition. Parry and threat is the logic of combat, in military tradition as in the boxing ring. You would not get very far unless you could do both. In military tradition, there is a strong emphasis on the need for an effective offensive as well as a defensive capability.

Even when the overall primary objective is clearly defence, there is a strong emphasis on the need for counter-attack. The army which remains within its defence is already defeated, goes the saying. If the objective is to *prevent* war altogether, or to 'deter' the enemy, then this tradition translates itself naturally into 'offensive deterrence' — deterrence by counter-threat, or by threatened counter-attack.

The military war-fighting sense of all this is perfectly clear, and indeed indisputable on the 'micro' scale. The difficulty with the counter-attack emphasis, however, arises when it is applied on the macro scale — when, in order to defend yourself, you pose a general or 'strategic' threat against somebody else's territory or military resources.

There are two problems which arise from such a posture. There is first the very obvious danger of *escalation*. The trouble with a counter-threat is that the threat part may be quite clear to the other side — but not the 'counter' part. Your opponent can easily see your counter-threat as a new threat *to which he has to respond*. Indeed, he may well be *duty bound* to respond, since it is the job of the military in all countries to defend their people against threats — and it is their job to be on the look out, to assume the worst, and not to be caught napping. This is called 'worst case analysis' — you have to prepare for the worst in order to be secure. If your opponent, like you, is into 'counter-threat' defence, and is also into worst case analysis, then his response to your counter-threat will obviously be yet another 'counter-counter-threat' — and so on. This kind of escalation obviously leads to instability,

Puzzle picture

insecurity and ever-increasing weaponry. If the objective of defence is security, that cannot be a good defence policy.

Deterrence by counter-threat is by its very nature ambiguous. A defence policy of this kind rather resembles those 'puzzle pictures' that you can see in two quite different ways — in this case either as offensive, or as defensive. Each interpretation of the picture is complete — it accounts for all the lines, and every line confirms it. If you screw up your eyes and turn a kind of mental somersault, however, you can suddenly see the other meaning — a meaning which is equally complete, which equally accounts for all the lines, and is confirmed by every line. The two perceptions are *discontinuous* — they do not gently merge into each other, they switch abruptly. and there is no question of one perception being 'right' and one 'wrong'. Both are right — and both are wrong.

The second problem with the 'counter-threat' type of defence is that it acts like a drug to limit perceptions. Defence by counter-threat tends to get people hooked on the idea of *balance* as being an essential aspect of defence — balance of weapon against weapon, force against force. Security is seen to depend on adequate counter-force — and therefore it can only be made stable as a 'balance'. Security is pictured as depending on a system of balanced and opposing forces. The image is easy to understand. It is rooted in nineteenth-century European history which we learnt at school and it is apparently scientific, fitting in well with a technological culture.

In sophisticated versions of the balance concept you have to have not only overall balance but balance at all levels of weaponry. Some people even assume that you have to have balance in expenditure — or in *rates of increase* in expenditure or in expenditure *as a proportion of the GNP* — an idea which has not even the remotest military justification.

The balance idea also has its own kind of escalation dynamics. Although it appears at first sight to be an image of stability, it clearly depends on people's *perception* of the weights on each side. As there is no way that the comparative weight can be objectively and scientifically determined, then there will always be dispute, and each side will 'for safety's sake' tend to underestimate their own weight and overestimate their opponent's. Meanwhile the military industry continuously offers new weights to rectify the balance. The dangers are obvious.

The balance of power

What then is the alternative? What other kinds of security systems are possible?

Let us go back to the basic problem of defence against attack. Defence by counter-threat is certainly one way to defend yourself: but it is *not* the only way.

Broadly speaking, there are four kinds of military response which can be made to offensive weapons. The first is to seek the means of destroying the enemy's offensive weapons — a *counter-force* strategy. A second is to defend your assets against the enemy offensive — whether by armour, fortification, obstacle formation or concealment. This can be called *obstruction*. A third is to remove the targets you present to the enemy offensive — i.e. to cease to present lucrative targets. This can be called *removal*. The fourth is to deter the enemy's use of his offensive weapons by threatening a similar offensive response. This can be called *offensive deterrence*.

In down-to-earth-terms, you fear an attack by armed gunmen, you can try to destroy or confiscate the guns of the gunmen (counter-force), provide for a counter-threat adequate to deter (e.g. by arming yourself), defend yourself by bulletproof/hiding etc. — or simply go away. Most of us in a real situation would go for a prudent mixture of all four.

If one of our major problems is escalation and arms race dynamics, then clearly we must give an added weighting at the macro level to other kinds of defence than the counter-threat ones — counter-force, blockage and removal. All these suggest ways of making an enemy threat ineffective without necessarily posing a counter-threat that is in any way comparable, or which can by any mental somersault be 'seen' as an offensive, and therefore justifying a counter-offensive response from the other side.

Real Defence

NATO actual defence posture in Central Europe is in fact a rather strange mixture.

Historically, one important element in this defence is nuclear weapons, which pose an offensive counter-threat. There are now between 5000 and 6000 battlefield nuclear weapons on the Central Front on the NATO side, consisting of nuclear artillery, anti-aircraft weapons and landmines. The reliance on nuclear counter-threat goes back to the days when the West had a near monopoly of nuclear weapons, and the natural way to deter an attack seemed to be to threaten massive retaliation with these superweapons if the East transgressed and crossed the border — the so-called 'trip wire' strategy. Not only did this seem the obvious policy, but it also was by far the cheapest. For some reason, it was not clear at the time that the Soviet Union would almost inevitably acquire the same kind of nuclear capability.

The 5000–6000 battlefield nuclear weapons are now mixed up with a conventional defence system which is a strange hybrid between offensive and defensive deterrence. It is not offensive in the sense that, taken as a whole, neither the equipment training nor deployment gave it sufficient clout to be able to invade Warsaw Pact territory — at present. On the other hand, the weaponry it deploys is in many respects rather more appropriate for offence than defence (as, of course, are those of the Soviet Union). In either case, the experience of World War II has been a dominating influence. In Germany, the Wehrmacht had originally been consciously armed for offensive war; and in the latter part of the war it continued to rely heavily on the tank offensive as an instrument for defence purposes. Something quite similar is true of the Soviet Army. The basic model for the postwar Soviet combat units was not the structures that had stood the test in the defensive battle up to Moscow after the Wehrmacht invaded, but rather those that had proved themselves ultimately in the offensive battles from the winter of 1943 on, and which gloriously and successfully 'rolled back' the frontiers in the 'Great Patriotic War'. Thus in West and East we are faced with units and structures that were really primarily designed for offensive assault. On the Western side, this pseudo-offensive force is designed for use in a cordon-type defence along the inter-German border, consisting of regular fighting units which will be moved up to their defensive positions in time of crisis. These units are contributed by five different NATO states, each taking a slice of the border in what is called a 'layer cake' structure. Behind this cordon there are scarcely any reserves to speak of, and a small, barely trained, infantry anti-tank capability.

In combat against attacking aircraft formations, the NATO position looks quite similar. There is a flimsy barrier with not much behind it. It is hoped that penetrating combat aircraft can be intercepted by the Hawk, the (nuclear) Nike and before long the (conventional) Patriot air defence cordon. If breaches are made in this cordon, the gaps can be guaranteed only by the very costly use of fighter aircraft. Potential targets deep behind the lines such as ports, traffic junctions, airports, etc., have virtually no air defence at their disposal.

What is generally agreed about the conventional defence posture is that it will not work very well in its present form. General Rogers, Supreme Allied Commander, Europe, gives it only 'a few days' in the face of a determined Warsaw Pact offensive.

In consequence, this defence has to fall back on the offensive counter-threat of nuclear weapons — especially the battlefield nuclear weapons which are used up with the conventional ones, and which NATO is allegedly prepared to use first if a conventional war is going badly. We are involved, therefore, in the prospect of the Supreme Allied Commander in Europe asking the political authorities for nuclear release within a week, and the political authorities having to choose between nuclear release and surrender. In the NATO Winter exercise

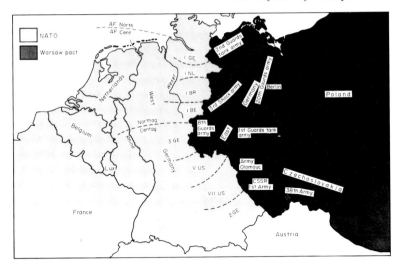

Combat formations on inter-German border

in 1985 this happened after six days. Since the Soviet Union now has the same kind of nuclear capability, and any nuclear use would probably escalate to an unmanageable holocaust, the West does not seem to be in a very sensible position.

Virtues of Defence

It is largely because of such problems that there has been a good deal of rethinking of philosophy and practice of military defence in Central Europe — particularly in Germany.

Much of the rethinking is about how best to defend this particular piece of territory in West Germany without threatening to blow up the world in the process. In making this exploration we are beginning to find that we are moving into a very rich vein of military tradition, and that in the security game of snakes and ladders we may well have found ourselves at the foot of a very long ladder.

It was Clausewitz who first established in military doctrine that the defence is intrinsically 'the stronger form of war', and his analysis still has a profound relevance.

RW-E

What are the essential differences in military terms between invading territory and defending it? First of all, and most obviously, the invading force is playing 'away', and the defender is 'at home'. This means that a defending force can make advance preparations on the battlefield of a kind which are impossible for the invaders. What Clausewitz calls 'the advantage of ground' lies naturally with the defenders, who possess the ground and are familiar with it. The ways in which the advantage of terrain contributes toward victory are fairly obvious. But it should be noted that this is more than a matter of obstacles to an attack — steep slopes, high mountains, marshy streams, hedges, and the like. Terrain may be just as useful by enabling us to hold a concealed position; even a featureless landscape can provide some advantage to those familiar with it.

Secondly, the invaders have to bring forward into hostile territory large quantities of men, firepower, equipment and supplies. Typically this is now envisaged, on the model of the last war, as a blitzkrieg-type operation based initially on a tank offensive with air support. The further the invader advances in hostile territory, the greater his problems become. Supply lines are increasingly extended and vulnerable. By initiating the campaign, the attacking army cuts itself off from its own theatre of operations, and suffers by having to leave its fortresses and depots behind. The larger the area of operations that it must traverse, the more it is weakened — by the effect of marches and by the detachment of garrisons. The defending army, on the other hand, remains intact. It benefits from its fortresses, nothing depletes its strength, and it is close to its sources of supply.

The problem of sticking your neck out in a hostile environment is increased by the attitude of the population. The defender has the natural support and obedience of the people, the invader does not; and although one single inhabitant of a theatre of operations has as a rule no more noticeable influence on the war than a drop of water on a river, the *collective influence* of the country's inhabitants is far from negligible. The defender can further capitalise on this advantage by enlisting a 'people in arms', or national militia.

Thirdly, and following directly from this previous point, invasion is *intrinsically* a much more visible activity than defence. Moving forward the paraphernalia of modern mechanised warfare into hostile territory is a high profile activity — and preparations for such an activity are also high profile. Destroying this equipment, and preparing to destroy it, can be a relatively low profile or stealthy activity. In Clausewitz's terms the defender's 'superior ability to produce surprise by virtue of the strength and direction of his own attack stems from the fact that the attacker has to approach on roads and paths on which it can easily be observed; the defender's position, on the other hand, is concealed and virtually invisible to his opponent until the decisive moment arrives'.

Against these intrinsic asymmetries which favour defence, we have to set the major asymmetry which favours invasion — that of taking the initiative. Invasion is an initiative, defence is a response. The invader can choose his time and place, the defender cannot. Clausewitz points out, however, that this advantage is a one-off affair. The one advantage the attacker possesses is that he is free to strike at any point along the whole line of defence, and in full force; the defender, on the other hand, is able to surprise his opponent constantly throughout the engagement by the strength and direction of his counter-attacks.

Clausewitz's argument is that these are instances of 'natural' advantages of the defence, and that in historical terms this means that even if the offence gains a temporary advantage, due say to the invention of a new weapon, the pendulum will always swing back and will tend to remain much longer on the defence side of the swing. When we look at the present problem of the defence of the West in a Clausewitzian perspective, we find that his 'natural advantage' not only applies today, but that we may well be able to take advantage of a massive swing in the defence-favoured direction.

So far as the *high profile* disadvantage of the invader is concerned, nothing could be more intrinsically high profile than the blitzkrieg-type tank attack which is feared in the West. Even the best of modern battle tanks are massive, noisy and heat-generating monsters, and have to be used in large numbers to have a chance of breakthrough. Strike aircraft, though much more rapid, have an even higher intrinsic visibility because they can be perceived from the ground against a contrasting uniform background.

This continuing and increasing high profile disadvantage of the invader has to be set in the context of a transparency revolution, in which we are all so deeply involved that we find it hard to see the wood for the trees. What is quite certain, however, is that what with the astounding advances in satellite surveillance that enables us to read car number plates from space, in television and fibre-optics which enables us to have thousands of eyes wherever we choose, and in infrared images and image intensifiers which make the night transparent, we are rapidly moving into a 'goldfish bowl' world where big fish will find it much harder to hide.

The twofold importance of this trend for the defence is obvious. First of all, increasing transparency can neutralise much of the advantage of the invader; surprise and initiative. As transparency increases, so surprise attack on any significant scale becomes more difficult. At the very least the attacker is forced to adopt complex deception plans (as did the Egyptians on the Suez Canal in 1973). These can only work in a situation of already heightened tension and confrontation. Secondly, transparency *selectively* favours the defender, who already has, as we have seen, a low profile advantage over the invader. The defender can be stealthier than the invader. This *potential* advantage is realised where there is *deliberate choice* of 'stealthy' systems by the defender.

The goldfish bowl world

It is not, of course, enough for the defender to be able to know what the offender is doing; it is also important to be able to stop him.

We therefore must also set the growing high-profile disadvantage of the *offender* in the context of extraordinary developments in *firepower* — the ability to project destructive force over a distance. A number of technologies are combining to produce more and more accurate, more and more lethal, more and more flexible and even portable systems for destroying unwanted objects. Thanks to micro-electronics, terminal guidance can be used to enable projectiles, both self-propelled 'missiles' and tube-launched 'shells', to home in on their prey. 'Fire and forget' missiles begin to replace the hazards of aiming; artillery gains a new dimension in accuracy; area bombardment weapons like multiple rocket launchers can make a quantum leap in discrimination and lethality. Thanks to explosives technology, armour protection can be pierced to ever-increasing depth and with increasing reliability. Although the development of armour protection is not standing still either, the balance of advantage has swung in favour of the technology of penetration rather than protection. Armour gives less mobility than it did. Moreover, we may well be approaching a situation when you could let people have in their broom cupboards (if they could be trusted!) weapons capable of disabling enemy armoured fighting vehicles.

The invader's highly visible activity is also a much more complex activity, and it becomes increasingly complex as the ability of the defender increases on the Clausewitzian down-gradient. The main battle tank (MBT) can, of course, be equipped with super armour, electronic counter-measures, instant fire extinguishers, more powerful engines, more advanced suspensions, and so on — just as the knights in armour could acquire more and more plate and bits and pieces — but at a cost, in numbers, reliability and weight. Modern Western MBTs are perhaps at the end of a line of development. They can get no heavier without losing the mobility that is the essence of their existence.

The same trends which are working against the use of armoured fighting vehicles are also operating against ships and aricraft. The Falklands War gave us a glimpse both of how much trouble even a poorly trained and not very well equipped Third World power could be to a medium power's fleet and of how a not very sophisticated aircraft could command the air using superior missile firepower. The effectiveness of the comparatively simple Sidewinder heat-seeking missiles against aircraft was no less impressive, if less publicised, than the performance of Exocet missiles against ships. The same kind of sombre lesson can be read in the history of the Middle East wars. Mobile weapons platforms are becoming increasingly vulnerable once detected.

We have then a situation in which advances in transparency and advances in firepower combine to return to the defence the natural advantage which Clausewitz predicted. But there is a third aspect of the present situation which is even gloomier for the aspiring invader.

To some extent, the natural disadvantage of the invader can always be remedied by speed. The *blitz* part of blitzkrieg has therefore become extremely important. In addition, all Soviet military doctrine stresses the importance of speed for any successful offensive against what is seen as an ill-prepared enemy, but an enemy with vastly superior potential resources. In Soviet eyes, to lose time is to lose the war.

The defender, however, who is playing at home, can make all manner of advance preparations to slow up mechanised forces which are in a hurry. The technology for doing this is of great variety, and is already widely available. They include some old-fashioned and low technology techniques like anti-tank landscaping and afforestation, constructing drainage ditches which double as tank traps, using explosive underground hose to create instant tank traps, prechambering bridges and motorways ready for instant demolition, and also highly sophisticated modern techniques like the most recent anti-tank mines.

These techniques and many others have been christened 'glue on the central front', and all capitalise on Clausewitz in the sense that they enhance the natural advantage of the defence. Many of the techniques involved are relatively inexpensive and there is no military commander who would not welcome a bit of glue.

The geography of the territory to be defended is also potential 'capital' for the defender who lives there and can make advance preparations. The Central Front must therefore be scrutinised with a defender's eyes.

Beginning in the south, there appears to be a possible point of entry for an offensive from the east out of Hungary and over Lower Austria. This line of attack seems impractical for several reasons. It is bad territory for tanks, easily defended, and the Soviet Union only has four divisions there in any case. Going futher north, an invasion from Czechoslovakia, where there are five Soviet divisions, the offence would have to be carried over the Bohemian Forest and the Bavarian Forest up to the Fichtel Gebirge, mountainous regions that are poorly or not at all suited for tanks. The offensive planners would have to take into account that a more or less intelligently waged defence would ensnare thousands and thousands of tanks at fordings, on steep slopes, in narrow corridors and roads, and wedged in between wooded areas.

We then come to the border between East and West Germany. Again from the Fichtel Gebirge to the Harz Mountains, forests, rivers and mountains provide good natural support for defence and limited options for attack. The 'Fulda Gap', the largest westward bulge in the GDR border, appears attractive to the Soviets as a gate of entry at best on maps that, as is not unusual in the USA, do not reproduce the terrain relief. In reality, especially on the GDR side, the Thuringian Forest presents a natural obstacle with very few passageways. And these could be blocked by the West.

North of the Harz Mountains, including the North German Plain there are indeed tracts of territory which at present seem to be an open invitation to an invader. When this territory is examined in the light of Clausewitz, however, the opportunities for effective defence are greater than has been assumed, and the natural advantage of the defender can certainly be exploited. Heath and moorland, woodlands, rivers and canals afford convenient obstacles. A cultivated landscape of fields and meadows surrounded by hedges, together with smaller woods frequently interspersed, provides cover for a geographically well-informed anti-tank defence. The enormous spread of low-density settlements, even urbanisation, of large parts of the borderlands over the past forty years has created further impediments. The advantage of the defender in urban warfare has been well established in military history and re-discussed in recent studies. Russians will remember that the ruins of Stalingrad were the grave of the German Sixth Army.

The geography of the East–West border does not of course in itself solve any problems. It is we who have to solve the problems. The geography, however, is our natural 'capital' as defenders — and if we want to be effective and it is this capital we have to exploit.

All these factors taken together suggest that the effect the blitzkrieg option could have against a well-prepared defence is of diminishing appeal. The initial breakthrough upon which the blitzkrieg depends becomes more difficult. Moves to improve assault potential often run counter to the surprise and long-range mobility aspects of classic blitzkrieg operations. So far as design of the Main Battle Tank is concerned, the conflicting needs for mobility, firepower and protection in an increasingly transparent environment tend to lead towards tank designs which have highly visible heat signatures, a massive logistical 'tail', and even so are not proof against all the latest anti-tank weaponry. So far as tactics are concerned, attempts have been made to rescue the blitzkrieg by marrying the tank assault even more closely with artillery, infantry and aircraft. All of these, however, run uphill against the natural advantages of the defender, enhanced by advancing technology.

Placing infantry in front of tanks, for instance, to 'sweep the path clean' for a following tank assault, carries a danger of reverting to the dynamics of 1914–18. It means exposing them to the same kind of dangers which made World War I such a static and bloody business.

When all these considerations are put together, we can begin to discover an emerging consensus about a new long-term option for the defence of the West in Central Europe. The shape of this defence can be summarised under the acronym FORT.

FORT — Forward Defence, Obstacles, Rear Area Defence, Transparency

F   *Firepower and Forward Defence*

Any invasion of territory must depend very heavily on the offender bringing forward a large quantity of 'mechanised force', including tanks, aircraft and armoured personnel carriers. This is by its nature a high profile activity, and it is essential for the defender to find the most appropriate means of destroying or disabling this mechanised force.

A forward defence zone needs to be established, not as a brittle wall designed to halt an invader, but rather as a thicket designed to disorganise and cripple him. It would ensure that penetration comes slowly and at a heavy cost, and that territory is not relinquished simply because hostile forces have crossed it; the waters should be ready to close behind the advancing force, cutting off his supplies and his line of retreat.

Firepower, especially anti-tank and anti-air, has a crucial role to play in this 'thicket' defence. Advancing tank formations present a relatively small number of discrete targets — an entire tank regiment, representing a quarter of a division's manoeuvre forces and covering a front several kilometres wide, has only about 150 major targets. They are tough targets. Even in good visibility, aircraft are hard-pressed to engage them, and with their mobility and hardness they are also very difficult targets for artillery. Even a typical battlefield nuclear weapon striking a normally dispersed tank company may kill only a few of its tanks. Soviet armour forces, however, are not without their vulnerabilities. By choosing tactics of rapid penetration instead of area control, the Soviets set the stage for defenders to engage their main forces and flanks with the carefully measured feints, leverages and thrusts of a karate defence (using the opponent's momentum against himself). Even more than most other tanks, Soviet tanks stress frontal armour at the expense of side and top protection. Soviet invading forces would take the classical gamble — that shock action can overwhelm a defender before he can take advantage of the attacker's exposed flanks and overextended logistic lines, or can bring his own military and psychological resoures to bear. It is impossible both to strike deep and retain flank security. A moving tank column cannot afford to sweep its flanks every time a shot is fired from the side, but such shots have the potential to destroy its effectiveness by killing its commanders and neutralising its minesweeping and air defence assets. Modern weapons enable defenders to engage tank-sized targets selectively from standoff distances up to 3 kilometres, by both direct and indirect fire weapons. Mortars firing anti-armour munitions with infrared or millimetre-wave homing sensors could wreak havoc on passing armour columns.

A tank screened by darkness, fog, rain, or smoke makes a very difficult target; but it also becomes very difficult for the crew, buttoned up in the protective armour of its vehicle, to follow what is happening outside, particularly to identify and engage flank targets. Under these conditions, tanks become very vulnerable to mines. Even simple systems of pulling mines across their route of movement can be very effective against tanks moving across hostile territory. Night or poor visibility also aids the defenders who can use radio warning nets and their superior knowledge of local terrain to choose vantage points for standoff attack. The use of road mines familiar in guerrilla war should not be neglected — and you don't have to be a hero to use them. Short-range anti-armour missiles could be developed into a simple roadside-emplaced, command-detonated mine which could engage selected targets with a relatively high degree of safety for the defender. Even the standard dual-purpose 40-mm round, now used with a variety of grenade launchers, could be adapted to flank attack with a small firing tube. Its 2-inch armour penetration capability would make it a deadly weapon against all Pact lightly armoured vehicles — personnel carriers, self-propelled artillery, tracked air defence systems, light tanks and command vehicles. High-velocity weapons in the 30-mm range could also be effective against tanks, particularly from the sides. Sniper and light weapons fire can ensure that armoured vehicles remain buttoned up, and also preclude use of external fuel tanks.

The deterrent effect of such thicket defence could be very substantial. The response of the invader must be to rely on artillery for softening prepared NATO defences, and to emphasise the protective role of dismounted infantry to 'sweep the flanks'; however, such actions can only be executed at the cost of rapid offensive manoeuvre, which is a paramount element of Soviet doctrine, and essential to winning the offensive.

Armoured vehicles also rely heavily and increasingly on resupply of ammunition and fuel. As tanks have increased in size and firepower, so they have doubly increased in dependence on a logistical 'tail'. In Soviet practice, supply columns follow behind armour thrusts, preferably moving at night or under conditions of poor visibility. Needless to say, such columns are extremely vulnerable to ambush.

The thicket cannot be confined to the ground; anti-air operations are a necessary complement to defence of the forward area. If invading forces control the air, then many of their disadvantages can be overcome. Aircraft, however, are intrinsically very 'high profile' objects, having a very distinctive 'signature' against the background of space. In the words of a leading authority 'Soon, if not now, any aircraft which climbs out of the nap of the earth into hostile radar vision within range of hostile surface-to-air or air-to-air missiles will be destroyed . . .' The only formations will be rotary winged ones. Outside the nap of the earth, both sides have total control of whatever air space they can reach.

O   *Obstacles ('Glue on the Central Front')*

Obstacles are the second important aspect of defence, either in the forward or in the rear areas. Since the defender is playing at home, he can make advance preparations on the battleground; and since any offensive relies on speed, the defender must capitalise on his ability to prepare the terrain in advance, and explore all possible ways of impeding forward movement.

Counter-mobility is a neglected study by the military which is only now coming into its own. A curious objection to any kind of obstacle formation is sometimes raised on the grounds that the 'Maginot Line' failed to keep the Germans out of France in 1940. This is an odd argument for neglecting preparations which all serious military thinkers would see as an important 'force multiplier'. In any case, the Maginot Line only defended the most vulnerable axis of German attack. It *successfully* diverted the German assault on to less potentially favourable approach areas, notably the Ardennes, along roads which could easily have been blocked. It was not the Maginot Line, but the Allies' manoeuvre defences that failed in 1940. To reject obstacles on Maginot Line grounds is a bit like saying you don't believe in having a front door any more because you were once burgled — through the back door! Moreover, there are equally valid historical examples of prepared defences, backed by mobile forces, blunting formidable armoured offensives, notably at Kursk in 1943 where armoured forces much more formidable than those of 1940 were quite literally stopped in their tracks by a system of interlocking anti-tank defences combined with mobile armoured reserves. Neither of the twin elements in this defence would have worked without the other, but the defensive or 'glue' element was essential in weakening the attacker before the decisive counter-stroke.

The counter-mobility weapons used so effectively at Kursk, were mines and kinetic energy anti-tank weapons, i.e. guns of various calibres. Both these types of weapon have a role to play in modern defences, enhanced as appropriate by new technology. Mines no longer have to be laid laboriously by hand in advance. They can be distributed by specially designed vehicles, artillery or rockets. 800 mines in a quarter of an hour is well within the capabilities of a modern mine emplacement team. Magnetic forces operate against the full width of enemy vehicles: no longer does the victim have to press on the fuse with wheel or track. New types of anti-tank submunitions fired by rockets can become effective anti-tank mines if they fail to detect a target on their initial descent. Dispensers of such weapons can also be emplaced, to be activated when they detect the correct signature of an armoured vehicle.

A whole new generation of anti-tank mines is now being developed. These include, for instance, mines which can work at a distance of 50 metres, can be set up only when the tank approaches, say from a ditch, a wooded area or grain field, and can be programmed for the number of tanks to be let through first. In defiles, these mines can be hand-laid by combat engineers, or can be shot from rocket launchers with ranges from 20 to 70 km, thus immobilising approaching tanks while they are still concentrating.

It is quite wrong, however, just to think of 'obstacles' in terms of sophisticated modern technology. After all, by far the best obstacles are the same as they have always been — the sea and the mountains, the rivers and the forests. It is essential for the defender to capitalise on and enhance all the obstacles which nature has bequeathed to him. Where these obstacles have been overcome by man, as for instance by roadways and tunnels and railway bridges, provision must be made for instant interruption of these facilities when they would favour an invader. It is also important to add to nature's obstacles and to imitate them wherever possible. Anti-tank 'landscaping' and afforestation could have an important part to play in a long-term strategy for making territory inhospitable to invading forces. Even quite young forests combined with an adverse slope can severely retard a tank offensive. Drainage ditches designed with a large vertical rise on the defender's side can have the same effect. Massive earth moving by JCBs and similar equipment is one of the most familiar and reliable techniques of modern society; its military potential could be exploited in ways which would in no way 'militarise' society, or even create visual eyesores.

Much of man's activity in Central Europe has already created formidable obstacles. The very dense pattern of towns and villages in the North German plain, for instance, has created many 'no go' areas for tanks. If a military dimension was added to town planning, these cultural man-made obstacles could be greatly enhanced, creating in effect a substantial pattern of obstacles and fortifications which would be quite invisible to the untrained eye.

Obstacle formation and counter-mobility is one of the oldest arts of warfare, and should again come into its own — provided, or course, that it is always seen as only one of the constituents of the FORT.

R *Rear Area Security and Defence in Depth*

The third element in an effective defence must be attention to the rear. It is above all the disorientating effect of movements in the rear (both material and morale), that create the conditions of success for blitzkrieg operations.

NATO's present defence is a bit like a shiny apple, rotten on the inside. Emphasis on forward defence has inhibited planning for operations within NATO territory, particularly in urban areas. In the immediate postwar period, the US nuclear umbrella protected European cities, while US strategic superiority ensured that the risk was low for US cities. The widespread lack of planning for systematic fighting within NATO territory would make an offensive attack easier for the Warsaw Pact, by easing its problems of consolidating control over any seized territory.

Security in the rear area is also weak. Few Western installations are hardened. Headquarters elements, telecommunications sites, support units, port facilities and storage depots (including fuel, ammunition, and equipment reserves) are at lightly defended locations well known to the Warsaw Pact. Clearly in the event of war the East plans to capitalise on these Western vulnerabilities. Hundreds of agents are either in place in Western Europe or could be infiltrated easily prior to hostilities and Soviet deep strike weapons and its sizable airmobile forces and operational manoeuvre groups are specifically trained for disruption of the NATO rear area. Transport could be rapidly disrupted, supplies cut off, reinforcements blocked and weapons destroyed.

Troops in the area are also largely unprepared for combat operations.

In the US infantry division, about half of the divisional strength consists of headquarters or support troops. They are required to fight as infantrymen when necessary; but this is usually taken to mean fighting as riflemen in perimeter security roles, or against small raiding parties. There is no combat organisation, and little training in the use of machine guns, anti-armour weapons, mines or explosives, particularly among the growing percentage of women soldiers. This means that tens of thousands of US troops can have only a small impact in direct combat.

This failure to establish proper rear area security and defence is the direct opposite of 'capitalising on Clausewitz'. It is above all in the rear area, if it does become a combat zone, that the defence has the most powerful advantage of playing at home, with all that that implies in terms of advanced on-site training and preparation.

The first step towards securing the rear should be a substantial upgrading of territorial forces, largely consisting of highly trained reservists, able at very short notice to undertake very specific combat tasks of the highest military utility. This is the opposite of the present system, whereby young men are 'called up' for a brief period of training on sophisticated equipment for use in frontal combat — equipment which they are never likely to see again as long as they live. Instead of being 'pseudo-regulars', most reservists should be highly professional irregulars — much more along the lines of the territorial forces of Norway, Yugoslavia or Switzerland. The Swiss in particular are able to conjure up within a day a highly competent territorial force.

The concept is not new. Immediately after the last war British Air Marshal Sir John Slessor strongly advocated such a defence. He argued for

'a highly trained semistatic Home Guard armed primarily with anti-tank guns with light automatics as the personal weapon. The Federal Republic . . . should be covered with a network of these units composed of local men, knowing every inch of the ground, every coppice and stream, lane and side street, responsible for the defence of their own town or village and inspired by the knowledge that they are protecting their own homes and their own kith and kin. They would be responsible for the storage and protection of landmines in peace and of laying the minefields when so directed

. . . . Their job would be to block every road and destroy every tank moving across country in their zone.'

If NATO countries in the central region followed the Norwegian example and mobilised all available current and former, active and reserve manpower resources, there would be an additional seven million troops in this critical area. West Germany, in fact, already has two million men in its General Reserve. These are not counted in its military manpower figures because they have no concrete defence assignment.

Closely associated with this upgrading of territorials and reservists is the idea of a universal *network* defence, which will be able to digest, entrap and destroy an invading force. The network implies a 'spider and web' structure — a marriage of largely local militia operating in their own home areas, with a highly trained and highly mobile regular force. The militia could be mobilised instantly, would not have to move, and so would remain largely invisible. They could merge back into the landscape as easily as they came out. Equipped with anti-tank and anti-air weapons, they could play a very significant combat role. Any such defence, however, must include highly mobile regular forces able to converge rapidly on any point of breakthrough and bringing force to bear on enemy forces which may have penetrated. In the view of Brigadier Richard Simpkin, this should involve a radical shift in military organisation. Rather than just thinking in terms of artillery support for regular infantry, or armoured forces, we need to recognise the increasing dominance of firepower by fielding new kinds of military formation with the specific task of bringing intense firepower to bear over a wide area and to be 'on call' like the fire brigade to neutralise any breakthrough.

Finally, rear area defence is likely to become even more important as the thicket defence of the forward area forces the Soviet military to explore the alternative of achieving surprise and rapid success by the use of airborne forces to take possession of rear areas while the massed tank forces in the East hold the attention of the main NATO defences. This could rapidly become the most significant Eastern option for 'winning' a war, and is something to which Western 'defenders' are bound to respond.

T   *Transparency*

The fourth necessary element in defence, the T of our FORT, is transparency. We have described three aspects of defence — Firepower, Obstacles, Rear area defence and security. None of these, however, makes any sense at all without what is referred to in military circles as 'C³I' — communication, command and control and intelligence. The set of activities constitutes the *brains* of the whole military activity — the ability to *perceive* what is going on, and the ability to *direct activity* effectively. Without C³I military activity would be like a chicken running round with its head off. The supreme importance of C³I applies just as much to the defence as it does to the offence.

As we have seen, however, the offender has a built-in disadvantage because he is engaged in an intrinsically high profile activity. It is intrinsically easier therefore for the defender to know what the offender is doing — provided, of course, the defender makes the right choice to capitalise on his natural advantage. It is also intrinsically easier for the defender to direct his own activities than for the offender to direct his. The defender is playing at home, and can therefore prepare his communication network in advance and on site, in a way that the offender cannot.

The task of the defender, therefore, is to enhance in every possible way the transparency of the goldfish bowl which the invader must enter, and ensure that his communication systems are effective and secure against disruption or attack.

Once again, the technological revolution is firmly on the side of the defender who makes the right choices. Though this subject is immensely complex in detail, it is worth mentioning just three aspects of technology which can immensely strengthen the defence.

First of all, techniques for satellite surveillance and reconnaissance drones for information gathering are advancing at a staggering speed. The entire surface of the earth can by surveyed in ever increasing focus of detail and by a *variety* of sensing devices. These 'eyes in space' are going to make any kind of surprise more and more difficult to achieve — and surprise is the one natural advantage of the offender. The supreme importance of these devices for identifying big strategic movements of military force is already widely accepted. (The fact that there is very little disagreement between the East and West about numbers of nuclear weapons is largely due to this.) Of course many of these systems are vulnerable — and will become more vulnerable if anti-satellite systems are not prohibited; but attacking your opponent's satellites is not a good way of achieving strategic surprise. At the tactical level, in addition, the importance of modern systems of surveillance and communication for close-in battle is also likely to increase dramatically as technology advances. Transmission of data, by fibre-optics for instance, makes it possible to conceal and 'harden' communication systems even against nuclear attack.

Secondly, the development of devices using near infrared and far infrared sensing systems is stripping away the traditional 'cover' of darkness and camouflage on which offensive action heavily depends. Already night-sights are readily available to infantrymen to enable them to shoot in the dark. Progress in this field, however, is extremely rapid. The next generation of surveillance, vision and sighting systems, in which the signals from various types of sensor will be combined and optimised by an image processor, will eliminate most of these problems. Moving and stationary military objects will then be as easy to 'see' round the clock in what we are used to thinking of as 'cover from view' as they now are in broad daylight in the open. In fact only dense forests of tall trees and built-up areas with tall buildings and narrow streets — environments in which it is difficult to move and impossible to carry out organised offensive action — will offer any certainty of concealment. Undoubtedly both passive counter-measures (clothing and paints) and active ones such as swamping heat sources, will be developed. But it is hard to see these overcoming the lead which thermal sensors have established.

Thirdly, it is essential to hold together the whole process of information gathering, and onward transmission of instructions, at whatever decision-making level is appropriate. The revolution in information technology, with which we are all familiar in our televised and computerised society, has brought about an equal revolution in military C^3I. Computer controlled electronic switching devices provide the basis for dispersed systems such as 'Rita' and 'Ptarmigan' that are both more capable and much less vulnerable than those of the past. All kinds of signals, including visual information and computer data, can

RW-F

now be transmitted with much greater reliability. This allows commanders fully to exploit computers to store, update and display the information required to run a complex and fast moving battle. The decentralisation inherent in the system allows a surprising amount of resilience to physical and electronic interference. Using modern position locating and reporting systems commanders no longer have to waste time finding out the positions of their own units — a serious difficulty not usually comprehended by the military layman. This puts the modern commander back in the position of the Napoleonic general who could run a relatively compact battle from a hilltop. Now his modern counterpart in relatively secure accommodation can run a complex, country-wide battle. If one headquarters is knocked out, back-ups are immediately available.

Of course, one must not underestimate the potential for confusion or disruption in any system of C^3I: indeed new technology opens up fresh avenues for compounding confusion. Yet there can be little doubt that the C^3I revolution gives at least the potential for coping with many of the most dangerous features of blitzkrieg operations such as its strike at the brain and nervous system of an opponent and its capacity to give its victims morale-crushing doses of surprise and insecurity. Now forces of all kinds can be more easily deployed to contain and then to crush enemy incursions. Moreover, Western superiority in electronics and computers (both hardware and software), combined with the Soviet military tendency to over-centralisation should give opportunities for superior Western offensive electronic warfare (EW) capabilities to disrupt the potential attacker's C^3I system which cannot be 'hardened' in the same way. This would further enhance the defender's opportunities to exploit the classic weakness of a blitzkrieg attacker, his vulnerability to outflanking and being defeated piecemeal.

Building Confidence

These four lines of approach summed up by the acronym 'FORT' are in no sense a blueprint or a set of magic formulae to resolve the problem of defence; but they do provide useful indications of the direction in which we should steer our ship. When we set our course, however, we also need to know what rocks to avoid. This means we need not just a defence policy, but a *security* policy. Let me explain what that means. Security is obviously a broader concept than defence. Indeed, the only sensible *objective* of defence policy is security. If security were not at risk, you would not need a defence policy. Defence, however, even thought of in purely military terms, is only one of two pillars of security. The second pillar is *co-operative security*. This term includes all those policies which are based on the assumption that East and West have *common* security interests and need to take *each other's* security into account. Co-operative security includes arms control, confidence-building and crisis stability.

This is a vast and complex area, but the general principles are clear and simple. As we come to recognise that armaments escalation, the build-up of weapons because of mutual threat, is *part* of the security problem — a statement that virtually everyone is now prepared to accept — then the *control* of this process must become an integral part of security policy. A defence policy which actually fuels the arms race, thereby causing in the long run greater insecurity, is quite obviously irrational, since it defeats the very objective which defence policy is intended to serve.

Crisis stability and confidence-building are now coming more and more to the fore in political debate between East and West, and quite rightly so. It is increasingly recognised that the greatest danger to peace may not be international war, but war as it were 'by accident'. The most likely accident would be one in which a crisis between East and West flared up, and either side misinterpreted the *defensive* reactions of the other side as being *offensive* preparations — something that could very easily happen. If, for example, the US nuclear bombers were ever to be launched as a precautionary measure in a crisis, this launch would immediately be picked up by the Soviet Union and would place them under immediate threat — to which they might well respond in kind. The worst danger is what is called 'pre-emption'. If you have cause to fear an immediate attack, then you are bound to 'pre-empt'.

A defence which involves the defender in taking actions in a crisis which inflame the crisis and which could give cause to the other side for a pre-emption, are obviously irrational defence policies, because when international tension mounts these defensive actions will be a cause of great insecurity.

In more general terms, a build-up of armaments over a long period which can be seen as potentially offensive to the other side — or which calls for or justifies responses of an offensive nature — is also counter-productive, because it helps to generate an arms race which destroys everyone else's security.

Defence policy and co-operative security policy are therefore complementary and inseparable. Both have as their objective the prevention of war. Defence policy prevents war by making it clear to a potential aggressor that he will not succeed. Confidence-building prevents war by effectively demonstrating that aggression is not planned anyhow. This provides a double safety-catch.

Confidence-building, in this general sense, must influence defence policy. In Central Europe, while security policy involves *emphasising* the kind of defensive systems we have described, it also involves *de-emphasising* the opposite kind of system. While we need to emphasise *more* 'area defence', much more effective short and medium anti-tank and anti-air systems, we also need to emphasise *less* our own tanks and aircraft capable of 'penetrating' the other side, and we need to place less emphasis on 'deep strike' technologies — weapons capable of firing deep into the territory of the other side, in order to destroy and disrupt the support system, the supply and the reinforcements, the communications system, the military bases. The emphasis, in short, should be on deterring an aggressor by having a visibly effective defence of the home territory under attack, rather than on counter-attack deep into enemy territory.

Of course, no military commander at the present time is going to consider for a moment abandoning in advance *all* possibility of attacking or firing beyond the international frontier in time of wars. This does not make any sense at all in military tradition, and for obvious reasons. If you can see an offensive being prepared or supported from a base over the border, you will as a military commander want to attack that base. Even under international law, which allows no other conceivable kind of warfare than a purely defensive one, there is an acknowledged right of 'hot pursuit' which entitles you to cross borders in pursuit of an enemy. General Rogers is therefore quite right to open a debate as he has done about 'Follow-on Force Attack', or 'FOFA' as it is commonly known. All the same, the *de-emphasis* on what we for shorthand describe as 'offensive' systems is just as essential as the *emphasis* which must be placed on systems which are 'just for defence'.

What is important about the present situation is that defence arguments and co-operative security arguments reinforce each other, and make it possible to construct two firm pillars of security policy, as a sound basis for common security.

Let us take *defence* criteria first in deciding what to avoid. Clearly we have to make choices. Money is certainly not unlimited, and we must make the 'best buys' in defence as in everything else. Even if a choice of direction has to be made, then from a purely military point of view there are some clear indications about the answers. There is not much point in planning to strike deep behind enemy lines if meanwhile you allow him to occupy your country. There is a lot of speculation about how the Soviet Union might attack in successive waves or 'echelons', lined up far back into Warsaw Pact territory waiting to exploit a breakthrough. In fact nobody can be sure whether there will be a second and third 'echelon', or where they will be if there are any — but we can be quite sure there will be a *first* echelon! Hamburg, Hanover and Nuremberg are all within 100 kilometres of the Soviet border, and as we have seen Warsaw Pact plans are for a rapid blitzkrieg-type advance, using 'Operational Manoeuvre Groups' to penetrate rapidly and deeply into NATO's rear area. Massed forces stacked up behind each other for hundreds of kilometres are not essential. If the Pact were to take Hamburg, Hanover and Nuremberg within a week with forces already near the border, then 'deep strike' would be of little avail except as a stepping-stone to nuclear war.

The first priority must be an effective defence against the first attack, and since resources are limited, choices will have to be made. Defensive systems ought to come before offensive: indeed General Rogers' FOFA proposals assume holding the initial Soviet thrusts as well as destroying reinforcements. Unfortunately we can't have area defence, deep strike and a build-up of existing types of forces all at once.

The second strictly military consideration which must give us pause in emphasising too much a deep strike approach is that striking deep into enemy territory, even by the most sophisticated modern technologies, does begin to involve you in some of the disadvantages of offence. By getting involved in very long-range and complicated systems, you are in a sense 'sticking your neck out', just as the invader does. Long-range systems have far more 'links in the chain' than short-range systems, and therefore, besides being much more expensive, are also much more vulnerable to disruption by a 'defender'. These are also much more fallible, and virtually impossible to test in operationally realistic situations. A few examples will help to illustrate this.

Multiple-launch rocket systems have been exalted as a means of delivering many explosive warheads which will crater and put out of action enemy airfields. The cost of doing this, however, escalates very rapidly with range. The missiles fan out with increasing range according to ballistic principles; and therefore if it takes x missiles to disable an area the size of a football pitch at 10 km, it takes $4x$ missiles at 20 km and $16x$ missiles at 80 km; and runways can be quite rapidly restored.

Assault breaker is another favourite 'deep strike' system, using the most sophisticated of modern technology. It is claimed that it can destroy tanks on the move deep in enemy territory. To achieve this, a long sequence of automated tasks has to be successfully carried out. A carrier missile is fired into the vicinity of the moving tanks; smaller sub-missiles are then dispensed and 'fly out'; after this they shed their fins and deploy parachutes; the remaining vehicle starts a motor which makes it spin and initiates 'search'; when it finds a suitable target it releases two 'Skeet' submunitions which attack the tanks. Because of the fallibility of each link in this long chain, the estimated probability of a Skeet killing its target is between 3.6 per cent and 4.5 per cent.

Of course, these systems will improve; but so will the means of destroying them — or deceiving them. A great deal of emphasis is placed on *VISTA* technologies (Very Intelligent Surveillance and Target Acquisition), and on *terminal guidance*. VISTA involves collecting and processing electronic data from many sources, such as radar sensors or remotely piloted vehicles, in order to pinpoint moving targets at distances of hundreds of kilometres, and predict their future positions. Terminal guidance involves programming missiles to search around and 'recognise' targets within a given search area or 'footprint'.

While all this is theoretically possible, the more extended the range the more the weapons systems rely on 'robotics' — on a long series of programmed responses. But robots, for all our science fiction, are merely slaves of their human masters; and in this case they are up against human beings who are determined to deceive them or destroy them. Possibilities of destroying, spoofing and deceiving robots are endless. Unlike robots, human beings are flexible, adaptable and can deal with the unexpected (which is what always happens in war). All links in the robotic chain are vulnerable. At the receiving end, obvious counter-measures against deep strike for moving vehicles would be speed changes, turns, firing of chaff, aerosols or flares either from vehicles or from automatic mortars.

In one known Soviet simulation technique, vehicles are made to appear moving down roads, when in fact there is nothing more than a line of small radar reflectors (to overload signal processing) and emitters (to attract fire) strung parallel to a road like Christmas-tree lights.

People who put their faith in 'emerging technology' to solve all these problems say that it was once thought impossible to put a man on the moon; but they forget that the moon was not trying to get out of the way!

While the deep-striker is forced to stick his neck out in extended robotics to reach further into enemy territory, the 'defender' enjoys the advantage of man-enhancing rather than man-replacing technologies. The natural advantage of the defender lies here with those who defend themselves against deep strike, rather than with the strikers. The more provenly effective ET systems are those with a 'man-in-the-loop' — like for instance the Russian SA8 'Gecko', which is a highly effective surface-to-air missile. The Gecko has a low light TV camera mounted on top of the tracking assembly to aim the missiles (which have infrared terminal guidance) against attacking aircraft; but the TV camera is manually operated.

If complex systems are deployed, not only are they more vulnerable, but they do in fact *invite* attack in a crisis situation. The destruction of guidance satellites in order to 'blind' the enemy then becomes a very high priority on both sides, since blinding the enemy is the only way to stop him killing you — and satellites, just like eyes, are highly vulnerable. Even the most non-violent of defenders would be inclined to throw acid into an assailant's face if this seemed the best way to stop him shooting you.

The defence argument becomes very much stronger, however, when the second pillar of security policy is taken into account — the need to take into account your opponent's security and probable reaction. Let us consider the situation for a moment as seen by the worst case in the East.

Let us imagine, for example, an ambitious programme for the development of deep strike technologies on the Western side; successful emplacement of conventional weapons able to strike and destroy key targets deep inside Warsaw Pact territory. Let us imagine that with a few high-precision hits on railroad bridges and switching areas, using advanced precision-guided conventional weapons, we can sever the lifelines of the Soviet's first line of defence in Eastern Europe. The nineteen élite divisions in the GDR are then left standing without reinforcement and supply. The material from the depots in Poland does not come through. A major part of the aircraft on the ground can be hit in or outside of shelters and neutralised with a surprise attack. The runways are destroyed, and time mines delay their restoration. Alternative airfields have no shelter protection.

Within a short space of time, the command centres required for waging conventional warfare can be put out of action by missiles, cruise missiles or aeroplanes. This means that within minutes or seconds Soviet troops in Eastern Europe can be left without central command. The emergence of popular uprisings, which are apt to tie down the Soviet forces in internal struggles, would then in Soviet eyes pose the gravest danger of all.

This may sound from the war-winning point of view as a very favourable situation. Seen from the Soviet point of view, however, it presents a major threat and fully justifies the deployment of similar deep strike forces on their side. Indeed, as we have seen, they are already far ahead of NATO in their ability to strike deep throughout Europe against military targets with their SS20s, 21s and 23s. Already some of these missiles are acquiring a significant conventional capability with improved accuracy and warheads (e.g. cluster munitions). We must assume that the Soviet Union would eventually match our advancing deep strike technology — and would have much less difficulty in in deploying it. This might be one answer to countering the new dispersed C^3I network. Certainly the existing links between the West's tactical nuclear weapons and the political leadership of the USA could be put out of action relatively easily. The threat to airfields would be especially severe. The AWACS bases would be unusable. NATO's other fixed assets would be at risk. There would be very limited potential for reconnaissance by means of aircraft or even reconnaissance drones. The operations bases of NATO air forces would be rendered useless and pipeline systems would be put out of action. Rail junctions for moving up Belgian and Dutch troops would be destroyed. The camps for the Rapid Deployment Forces from the USA would be rendered unserviceably. NATO's conventional combat units in the Federal Republic would face tremendous deployment problems, their command centres would largely be paralysed. Within a few hours the initial loss in combat strength would be irreplaceably great.

A wrong choice of direction in new conventional technologies could therefore reinforce the trend whereby the one who strikes first can gain enormous advantages which his opponent can no longer offset. The difficulty with such a system is that it is both highly unstable in crisis, and also that it is highly malignant to arms control which is an essential component of confidence-building. The movement towards 'deep strike' provides a strong justification for a 'balanced' offensive response, or at the very least for counter-force weapons that will disable the enemy's weapons in the first stages of conflict. In a crisis situation, both sides tend towards the situation of two gunfighters in a wild Western. The one who is quickest on the draw 'wins'. That is not a good recipe for security.

This does, of course, leave the West with a defence problem. The East already has some substantial deep strike capabilities against the West. The Soviet Union now has a whole new generation of deep strike missiles deployed in East Germany and in the Soviet Union. As stated above, these include not only the infamous SS20s, but SS21s, 22s and 23s, with ranges of 75, 560 and 300 miles respectively. Part of the Soviet 'response' to the final NATO agreement to deploy the comparable Pershing II and Cruise nuclear missile was to move forward the long-range SS22 into East Germany. From locations in East Germany, this missile extends Moscow's 'short-range' missile coverage to NATO's rear areas, including bases in the United Kingdom.

A quick look at the map reveals just why these new missiles are so different. Most of NATO's highest value military installations (nuclear weapons sites, airfields, air defence sites and storage depots) — a few hundred in number — are located within 300 miles of the inter-German border. Based in Eastern Europe, the new Soviet missile could easily reach these critical installations. And, while conventional and chemical warheads are by no means as effective as nuclear weapons, most of these targets could still be effectively attacked by non-nuclear missiles because the installations are unprotected.

If the West is seeking to avoid a similar deep strike build-up in the overall interests of security policy, then what can the West do about *defence* against these weapons? What is to stop the Soviet Union using its deep strike capability against Western Europe — or at least threatening to use it — and thereby 'winning a war'?

The answer to this question in purely defence terms must be to explore the other forms of defence which are available. If you are threatened by a weapon you can defend yourself by counter-threat, by protection, by counter-force, and by removal. Counter-threat in the sense of 'threatening the like' is not only contrary to crisis stability and arms control, but it is not a defence either, since the 'first striker' would still win. We are necessarily obliged, therefore, to think of the other kinds of defence.

Protection and counter-force go hand in hand. Certainly the West will have to move towards 'hardening' key military sites, and towards defending them against aircraft and missile attacks. One of the most important positive results of the Star Wars programme may well be the development of limited systems of defence against 'tactical' missiles in Europe. Whereas no one believes that a complete defence can be developed to cover, say, the USA against a massive nuclear attack, there are strong indications that it would be possible to defend a number of key military targets in Europe against deep strike missiles, whether nuclear or non-nuclear. This is an important line of research which must be pursued, though not without taking into account the implication for confidence-building and arms control.

The key to this problem, however, may well lie in that fourth mysterious category of 'removal' — going away, or ceasing to present lucrative targets. Ceasing to present lucrative targets is in fact the natural by-product of effective defensive deterrence along FORT lines in Western Europe.

The defensive system itself, in the area of combat, can be constructed as a network system which presents no significant targets either to the enemy airforce or artillery. The move away from tank-heavy mechanised units is also a move away from presenting lucrative targets. If we have a defence which is decentralised, dispersed, which involves the local population, capitalises on initiative, and has 'hardened' and multiple communication networks, then we are capitalising on Clausewitz to reduce our profile, and therefore defend ourselves against enemy firepower.

As regards the capability of Soviet missiles to 'strike deep' against military and industrial targets throughout Europe, we clearly cannot 'remove' these targets in the physical sense.

However, these are *only* perceived as lucrative targets by the Soviet Union if a successful offensive can also be carried out on the Central Front. There is not the slightest point in striking deep unless you can also as it were successfully strike shallow — the same conundrum which the West faces in having to choose between deep strike and defence in the battle area. A deep strike against Europe without a successful assault on the Central Front would be pointless. As the West moves, therefore, towards effective defence deterrence in Europe, it will automatically take care of part of the problem which it perceives of being 'under the shadow' of a protentially hostile superpower.

There is, however, another aspect of this problem which relates to nuclear weapons as a whole. That we must deal with in the following chapter.

The black aces

3
Ritualising Nuclear Weapons: I. Strategic

Strategic nuclear weapons are like the head of a dragon. They are the major nuclear systems with which each side can destroy the other. The dragon also has a body and a tail, which I shall talk about in the next chapter. But first it is necessary to take a good look at the head which animates the body.

The nuclear arsenals of the East and West at present cancel each other out. It was the American Defense Secretary Robert MacNamara who coined the grisly term 'MAD' (Mutual Assured Destruction), to described the relationship between the superpowers. He meant that nuclear weapon capabilities on both sides were such as to ensure that totally 'unacceptable damage' would be inflicted on either power if it actually used a weapon in its possession. In other words, there could be no winners in a nuclear war.

If you were to make up a card game in which 'black ace always wins', that could work satisfactorily — although it would put an end to all the fun of playing cards. If, however, there turned out to be *two* black aces, one of each opposing side, the game would go on as before. No one would play his black ace, but no one would discard it either. The two would simply cancel each other out.

What Robert MacNamara described as 'MAD' in the 1960s is even more true today, with something like a million Hiroshimas shared between the two opposing sides and no effective defence against them.

Why then should we worry?

Although MAD is a fair description of the situation in which the world finds itself, nothing could be madder than to think we could as it were rest on our MAD laurels.

It is important to remember that MAD was not a clever doctrine or policy that some statesmen thought up to secure peace. It was not a doctrine, but a description of the situation. The situation it described was that the Soviet Union, having lived for fifteen years under the threat of 'massive retaliation' from the USA if it transgressed, had now got its own means of massive retaliation — its own black ace. MAD was not a doctrine that produced a deployment, but a deployment that produced a doctrine. Of course, each side would greatly prefer the other not to have its black ace. There was certainly never any clear policy commitment to MAD on either side. The nearest approach to such a policy commitment was the ABM treaty in 1972 — the treaty by which both sides agreed severely to limit its means of *defence* against the other missiles. This was an attempt to establish the 'mutual hostage' idea. But the treaty itself was only possible because defence against nuclear weapons at that time seemed *impossible*. Neither side really committed itself to the mutual hostage idea as a guide to defence policy. Far from it. Every means possible was explored of depriving the other side of its black ace — and it would be quite extraordinary if it were otherwise.

It is this continuing dynamic of the arms race which makes it exceedingly dangerous to rely on a vague idea of Mutual Assured Destruction for any reassurance about long-term security. At the best, it is a leaking boat which is in urgent need of repair if it is to get us to a safe port.

What has happened to MAD in the context of developing technology is quite clear. One might have thought that 'enough was enough', and that once each side had sufficient weapons to eliminate the other the race would end. This, however, is not the case. The strategic weapons are *developed*; they become more accurate and versatile, and the pressure to deploy the improved strategic weapons is immense. As the strategic weapons develop, a new possibility emerges, that of using them against the enemy's strategic weapons, and his other military installations, using them, that is, for a first strike, which will eliminate the enemy's power to retaliate. Other technological developments help this process forward — especially anti-submarine warfare, by which the enemy's power to retaliate can be limited, and anti-ballistic missile systems, which can reduce the damage done by nuclear retaliation. Once this possibility of attacking the other side's nuclear weapons is foreseen, then the pressure to do so is immense, and the better you can do this, the nearer you are to a first strike capability. Once the drift towards first strike is in motion, each side is almost bound to go along with it — if only to stop the other side getting there first. This means, of course, a colossal build-up of strategic weapons, so that enemy missiles can be 'saturated' — or so that you can avoid your own being saturated and still respond with a 'second strike' sufficient to deter. The Soviets and the Americans both see themselves and each other in one of those two situations at the present time.

It may well be that neither side actually *intends* to develop and use a first strike capability. It is also almost certainly true that first strike is a pure mirage — nobody will ever get there. As in all warlike interactions, however, *it is the meaning that matters*. First strike advantage tends to acquire a meaning of its own. Once the possibility exists, you are almost bound to become involved in a first strike race. If you suspect the other side of going in this direction, then you will take counter-measures like developing anti-ballistic missile systems and multiplying your own missiles; all these defence measures, however, *could* mean that you are *yourself* drifting or even steering towards a first strike advantage, and therefore to a position of dominance.

There can be no doubt that we have, as a human race, got ourselves into an extraordinary predicament. Forty years ago the first atom bombs were dropped on Hiroshima and Nagasaki. We had invented a weapon so horrific in its effects that it changed the vocabulary of war,

The sorcerer's apprentice — twentieth century

dividing history in the 'pre-nuclear' and the 'post-nuclear' ages. It also applied a goad to the conscience of the human race that can never be removed. Forty years on, here we are with over a million Hiroshimas in our stockpile, and we are still busy 'improving' that stockpile by adding new weapons every day.

Some people think that what is going on is just some automatic process, and that whatever we do, weapons will continue to be churned out by what President Eisenhower called the military–scientific–industrial complex', just like the broomsticks in the 'Sorcerer's Apprentice'. This is a somewhat gloomy view. We must remember, however, that eventually the Sorcerer returned to pronounce the right 'spell' (or *word* — and the word put the broomsticks to rest). We should never underestimate the importance of words. Of course, human history has as its raw material a number of 'automatic' processes over which we seem to have little control. But human history is a quest for meaning, and it is only by getting a grip of this meaning that we can gain control. We must find the right 'spell'.

What might this 'spell' be?

Let us think first of all about the big weapons — the 'strategic' nuclear weapons. These are the most obviously 'MAD' of all nuclear weapons, in that any substantial use of them at present would trigger a retaliation which would destroy the homeland of the first-user. They are also the most MAD in the second sense, that they would be the most likely to generate a nuclear winter which would destroy the rest of the world as well.

What we have to do is to make sure first of all that the MAD *does not change in a way that makes the situation more dangerous than it is at the moment.* This means, of course, accepting that MAD makes some kind of sense — relatively speaking. It may not be everyone's ideal, but everyone will agree that we could go 'from MAD to worse'. Worse could be, for instance, a first strike capability on our opponent's side. Nearly everyone would agree with that. More enlightened people, who can see a structural and interactive problem, would agree that first strike capability on *our* side would also be worse — either because of the temptation to use it, or the provocation to the other side to pre-empt. Even worse would be first strike capability on *both sides simultaneously* — not at all an impossible situation. Imagine two opponents with a revolver held to each other's heads!

There is, therefore, some sense in MAD, relatively speaking. But let's not call it 'Mutal Assured Destruction' any more. What we are concerned with is Mutual Assured Deterrence, or even better, the French equivalent 'Mutal Assured Dissuasion'. As long as dissuasion is assured, then the system works. Threatened destruction may be one way of doing this — but it is a means, not an objective. Dissuasion and destruction are not the same thing; you can dissuade without threatening to destroy, and you can threaten to destroy without dissuading. Some people are not even dissuaded by destruction (e.g. highjackers)! The fact that we are stuck at present with a high destruction content in the dissuasion part of MAD should not obscure the fact that it is dissuasion and not destruction which is the objective.

Something we have to do is to steer this leaky vessel of MAD, in

RW–G

It takes two to tango!

which we find ourselves drifting, and make sure it does not land us up on the rocks of first strike. How is this to be achieved?

One thing is quite clear. We can only stop the first strike drift *in co-operation* with the other side. In the hackneyed but still cogent cliché of arms control, 'it takes two to tango'. The reason for this is simply that a drift by *either side alone* towards first strike is highly dangerous.

If it were possible to block the other side's first strike drift, without drifting the same way yourself, that would be fine, of course. That was one of the original hopes of Star Wars. President Reagan had a noble vision of a world in which nuclear weapons would become impotent and obsolete, because we would be able to construct a 'magic umbrella' of strategic defence against incoming missiles. His instincts were right — we do need to make nuclear weapons impotent and obsolete, and SDI could indeed be one way of achieving this. But apart from the practical difficulties of constructing the magic umbrella, the real problem is that by putting up even a partial shield and *keeping your sword* — your own offensive nuclear weapons — you drift nearer *yourself* to a first strike posture; you seem to be getting into a position where you can 'zap' the other side's missiles, and not fear retaliation from the few that are left! Of course, if the other side co-operated, you might be able to synchronise your defensive deployments; but then, if you can tango as well as that, you might just as well tango the offensive weapons away in the first place, and then you would not need your strategic defence!

So we have to accept at this stage that East and West are in the same boat together. That does not mean, of course, that the only way forward is through formal negotiations and elaborate treaties. There are other ways of co-operating. There are lots of ways to tango. But it always takes two.

There are three broad principles which must be observed if we are to put an end to the first strike drift. The first principle is negative — what we must steer *away* from; the second positive, what we must steer *towards*; and the third is a kind of 'rule of the road' to help us negotiate rocks and obstacles in the way.

The first principle is *First Strike Avoidance* — to avoid or prevent all developments which lead in a first strike direction. The second is *Reductions* — to steer towards less nuclear infested waters where first strike becomes increasingly remote. The third is *Equality* between the superpowers — a rule of the road without which the most well executed tangos are likely to degenerate into an unsightly brawl. Let us take these three principles in turn.

What do we have to avoid first of all, in First Strike Avoidance? Clearly we must avoid cancelling out either side's means of *dissuasion*. We are at present in a situation of Mutual Assured Dissuasion, and to stay alive we have to assure *each other's* means of dissuasion.

The magic umbrella

For the time being, unfortunately, our primary means of dissuasion is each side's highly destructive strategic nuclear weapons aimed at each other's 'assets'. We have, therefore, a common interest in ensuring the *invulnerability* of these weapons systems. If each side has an invulnerable retaliatory capacity sufficient to dissuade, then Mutal Assured Dissuasion is effective. This invulnerability has two aspects to it.

First of all, the retaliatory systems of both sides must be *survivable* — i.e. able to survive any likely offensive from the other side at least for sufficient time to counter-attack; and secondly, the second strike systems of both sides must be *effective* — they must indeed present an unacceptable mutual threat. In this respect one of the spin-offs from the SDI programme could be a better point defence of some of your own retaliatory systems. That is much more feasible than the magic umbrella and indeed to a limited extent is permitted by the ABM Treaty; but it is in fact part of the *opposite* concept — the very mutual hostage idea that President Reagan wished to eliminate.

Survivability is not just to be thought of in terms of protecting weapon systems. Even more important is protecting the *control* systems — the command headquarters and the communication network that is the effective 'head' of the whole system. Decapitation has for long been the main risk to the nuclear superpowers and their most dangerous temptation in a crisis. As long as it is possible for either or both sides to paralyse the other by decapitation, then the dangers in a crisis are very great; and to respond to this danger by 'launch-on-warning' is to jump out of the frying pan into the fire! What we need is a retaliatory force so secure that there is no hair-trigger on either side.

A number of arms control principles follow from such a commitment. The stationing of missiles close to enemy borders should be prohibited, to reduce the decapitation option; any forward deployment of Cruise missiles could be prohibited (whether on the land or at sea) for the same reason. Submarine-launched strategic missiles remote from enemy shores should, however, be in a privileged category, since they are the most survivable second strike systems — the oceans being the last hiding place left on earth. Undersea command posts could be created to make sure that the submarine system would be able to keep its 'head'; and submarine sanctuaries could be created to prevent attacks on either side's submarine-based deterrent.

This policy involves a big change of thinking on both sides, and it is not surprising that it is proving difficult. The quest for invulnerability, survivability and effectiveness of *one's own* weapons systems and communication systems clearly fits with all the military and defence traditions. A major aspect of the evolution of strategic nuclear systems for instance hardened silos, mobile land systems, submarine systems, has always been 'survivability'. What is totally at odds with the military and defence traditions, however, is the concept that invulnerability is desirable *on both sides*; that the most secure situation is one in which not only your own strategic weapons but also those of your adversary are both secure against your weapons, and guaranteed to be effective against targets your own side (other than against your strategic weapons systems). On the contrary, the desirability of being able to defeat the enemy in war if it is possible to do so is so natural and inevitable a part of all military tradition, whether Eastern of Western, that any principle which goes directly against such a tradition would be virtually impossible to impose unless extremely powerful contrary pressures could be mobilised. The principle of the *invulnerability* of the *enemy's* forces, and the *vulnerability* of *your own* assets is just such a principle. Yet unless such principles are accepted as guiding principles which will actually influence defence policy and deployments, it is very hard to see how the endless drift towards the mirage of first strike can possibly be avoided, with all its attendant dangers.

The pursuit of invulnerability or survivability of one's own systems can and must be given a high priority regardless of the strategic priorities of the other side; but progress towards maintaining the effectiveness of the opposing system can only be achieved through negotiations and then only on the basis of an extremely firm and clear commitment in principle, strong enough to override the military pressures moving in the opposite direction.

The basic postulate on which agreement must be reached (and has indeed been formally reached at the Gorbachev–Reagan summit in 1985) is that strategic nuclear wars are not winnable. There is already a very substantial body of thought on both sides which declares this to be the case; but on both sides there is also ambivalence, with nuclear war-winning strategies competing with the concept that nuclear war is unwinnable. Once the unwinnability of strategic nuclear war is firmly declared and established, it must then become the guiding principle of strategic arms control, and it must be accepted that this doctrine, already accepted as a legal principle in SALT I, marks a clear break with all established military and defence traditions.

Many directions of exploration become feasible once the basic principle of survivability is accepted.

Reduction in Numbers

Reduction in numbers of strategic nuclear weapons, although commonly and correctly accepted as a desirable negotiating goal, is less obviously connected with Assured Strategic Deterrence than invulnerability. It could well be argued that large numbers on both sides in themselves strengthen deterrence, since thay make a first strike less probable, by increasing the number of targets which a first strike must eliminate.

However, large and increasing numbers of weapons are not, as we have seen, a guarantee against first strike, since the increase in accuracy of strategic weapons is likely to outpace the invulnerability due to numbers alone; and in this situation, the numbers race becomes part of the first strike race, and is therefore destabilising. That does not automatically mean that less numbers would necessarily be more stable. Indeed, reduction in numbers alone could lead to a more dangerous situation, if the remaining weapons were adapted to a first strike. A small number of MIRVed and accurate ICBMs on each side, for instance, could constitute a first strike capability on both sides, and this would be a highly unstable situation, inviting pre-emption in a crisis. Reduction in numbers, therefore, only makes sense *when combined with the principle of invulnerability*, and when the reduced deployments are based explicitly on the principle that nuclear war is unwinnable.

With this proviso it is clearly in the long-term interest of arms control and stability to aim at substantial and progressive cuts in numbers of strategic nuclear weapons. There are two basic reasons for this. First, it is in general true that the greater the numbers, the more difficult the system is to control and the greater the danger of accident. Second, the instability and the cost of nuclear deterrence is now such that unless rapid and controlled reducing momentum is soon initiated, and then continued towards a Minimum Assured Strategic Deterrent, we are heading for very turbulent waters and could well be shipwrecked on the rocks of a pre-emptive nuclear strike.

Equality

The third guiding principle of all arms control, 'the rule of the road', must be equality between the superpowers.

It is even less obvious from the military point of view why equality is important in a defence perspective than reduction in numbers. There is now a commonly held view that for deterrence purposes both sides possess massive *over*kill and there is no point in adding further strategic weapons as it were to 'bounce the rubble'. In theory, therefore, from the pure deterrence point of view, it should be possible to ignore equality in the first phase and make drastic cuts without reference to cuts on the other side.

There are two problems to this approach.

The first is that it ignores the first strike drift — the perception on either side that the other is moving towards a nuclear war-fighting advantage. This stimulates an arms race in which numbers are highly relevant. Substantial one-sided cuts would be inconceivable if they increased the nuclear war-fighting advantage of the other side.

Even more important, however, are the political and legal perspectives which have made the pursuit of equality a fundamental 'Common Law' of arms control negotiations. As we have seen, it is only through negotiation that substantial progress can be made in strategic reductions; and both sides are publicly committed in their negotiations to the principle of equality. This principle has become symbolic of the 'bipolar balance' structure which is an important element in the perceptions of both sides. In the long term it is probably the only structural image which can be used to counteract the rival image, which is that of world domination by a single superpower, associated with the pursuit of nuclear superiority. The principle of equality is therefore both necessary and desirable and could never be abandoned by either if that implied or appeared to imply a formal acceptance of inferiority.

These three principles, therefore — invulnerability, reductions, and

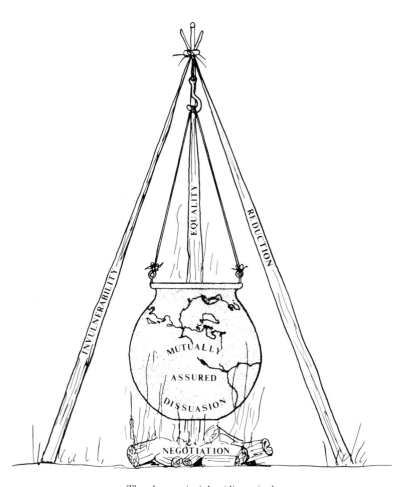

The three principles 'dissuasion'

equality — must constitute the tripod on which all arms control efforts are based in the move towards Mutual Assured Dissuasion.

On the basis of such principles, there is no reason at all why we should not begin to develop a 'common language' of arms control between East and West. Establishing a 'common language' of this kind need not lead back into an endless swamp of protracted and abortive arms control negotiations. We can, however, learn a great deal from our previous incursions into the swamp. We must ultimately transform the 'nuclear balance' into a ritual, in which the operational use of these weapons becomes more and more remote, even to vanishing point — though their *meaning* remains. If we can achieve this, then we shall have reached a watershed in the quest for security in the nuclear age.

4

Ritualising Nuclear Weapons: II. Battlefield and Intermediate

The Link

So far we have only been talking about the major nuclear weapons systems of the two superpowers — the so-called 'strategic' nuclear weapons. In a sense, however, these are the least of our problems. It is the smaller ones that are our biggest problem.

I said at the beginning of the last chapter that strategic nuclear weapons are like the head of a dragon — a dragon which also has a body and a tail. In this section I would like to take a look at the body and the tail of this monster. The tail consists of a mass of 'small' nuclear weapons littered around the projected nuclear 'battlefield' in Central Europe — places close to where they would be used in the event of a nuclear war and where they are closely entwined with conventional weapons. The body of the dragon is the 'intermediate' nuclear weapons, which fill the gap between the battlefield ones and the strategic ones — weapons like the Russian SS20s, which can be fired from Eastern Europe and hit military targets in France, England and Italy, or like NATO's Pershing IIs in Germany, which can reach the western Soviet Union and probably Moscow within ten minutes. What is the *rationale* for these less than strategic nuclear weapons? How do people think about them in relation to the big strategic nuclear weapons? Are they just part of the MAD set-up, or are they something quite different?

The purpose of less-than-strategic nuclear weapons is in general seen as forming a *link* between the nuclear weapons of the superpowers and the battlefield in Europe. It is the nature of this 'link' which presents us with the great conundrum of defence policy. Resolving this conundrum could be the key to resolving the problem of war in the nuclear age.

First of all, it is important to understand why people come to believe that a link between MAD and the battlefield is necessary. There are two basic reasons for this. One is to do with protecting allies — the need for a so-called 'umbrella'; and second, much more profound, is to do with the problem of war in a nuclear age.

First of all, there is the question of the umbrella. So far as the superpowers are concerned, it is not too difficult to imagine procedures and rules of the game which would help them to establish *between each other* the unusability of nuclear weapons. They could conceivably agree to move towards invulnerable, second-strike-only systems, to seek equality rather than superiority, and disentangle nuclear weapons from the battlefield. The problem is, what then happens to the superpower *dependents*? In particular, what happens to Western Europe? What happens to West Germany? What happens to the 'umbrella-ed' powers — that is to states, other than the USA, who see themselves now protected by a 'nuclear umbrella'?

The difficulty is this. The more the superpowers progress towards ritualising nuclear weapons and the less usable nuclear weapons become as between them, the less can they then be seen as an umbrella for third parties. This leaves third parties in theory wide open to nuclear blackmail. In particular, it leaves Western Europe wide open to nuclear blackmail by the Soviet Union.

There is no escaping this dilemma in military terms. The turbulence that has afflicted Europe over INF deployments, whatever its immediate cause, can be seen as an almost inevitable result of the progress toward MAD achieved in the SALT process. The very fact that the nuclear systems of the two superpowers become increasingly unusable against each other can mean they can become *more usable* in relation to third parties. If the USA cannot be expected to commit suicide for Europe, then Western European countries are exposed.

The second reason why many people believe there must be a link between nuclear weapons and the battlefield has to do with the deeper problem of making sense out of nuclear weapons.

Let us imagine for a moment that we could *totally* decouple nuclear weapons from conventional weapons. Let us imagine that we establish a total and watertight 'mutual nuclear deterrent' between East and West, so that the nuclear system really does become *quite irrelevant* to any other form of warfare or preparation for war between the superpowers (much as it is already irrelevant to the conflict in Nicaragua or Afghanistan). Where would we be in terms of world order and world security?

The answer must be that in that situation (which is purely hypothetical) we should have 'made the world safe for conventional war', in a way that it is *not* safe now. There is very little doubt that the great caution observed by the superpowers in relationship to any military conflict with each other is due to a large extent to the presence of nuclear weapons — nuclear weapons which are not in a watertight compartment. These weapons are seen not just as cancelling each other out but also as putting a dampener on *all* war between the superpowers. This is not just abstruse strategic theory, it is downright commonsense which anyone can understand.

Beneath this perception is an even deeper one, and an even broader one, a perception which is often shared alike by anti-war protesters and by like establishment. This is the perception that nuclear weapons, through their very obscenity and uselessness for winning wars, are presenting the human race not just with the problem of nuclear war, but with the problem of *all wars*. To separate off the two issues into totally watertight compartments is therefore in a sense to fail to respond to the challenge which history presents to us.

Problems of Linkage

How on earth can we conceive this 'link' between MAD nuclear weapons of the superpowers and the practical defence of Europe? The underlying difficulty is that conventional weapons are seen as usable, and nuclear weapons in the MAD context are not. Trying to stick them together is rather like trying to pin apple jelly on the wall.

Let us take a quick historical look at some of the difficulties we have got into, to see if we can learn from them.

Battlefield nuclear weapons in Europe began their life as quite usable weapons. They were first deployed in large numbers on the Central European front by NATO in the 1950s, when the USA still enjoyed a monopoly. They were seen as a highly effective and relatively cheap operational deterrent to counter the build-up of Soviet conventional weapons in Eastern Europe. They could be used with devastating effect against massed Soviet tanks and troops, and when backed by a vastly superior US strategic force they could constitute a credible and effective defensive deterrent. Even when the Russians acquired their own strategic weapons, they still retained credibility since their use by the West would be unlikely to trigger a suicidal Soviet strategic response.

However, from the very beginning doubts were expressed about the military usefulness of these weapons, and these doubts have steadily increased to the present day. Indeed, many experienced military officers, such as General Maxwell Taylor and Admiral Noel Gayler, have stated that they were unable to devise plans for using battlefield nuclear weapons.

First of all, any use of these weapons would cause massive collateral damage which would inevitably affect the defenders as well as the aggressors. Their use in Western Germany would be devastating to friend and foe alike; even a modest tactical use could involve one million immediate German casualties, most of them civilians — with a highly problematic effect on alliance cohesion.

Secondly, it was impossible to acquire targets in any way proportionate to the destructive power of massed nuclear artillery; and surface-to-air nuclear missiles would blind any fighter pilots in their vicinity, whether friend or foe. In addition, some of the weapons have become obsolete. The atomic demolition mines had to be buried deep underground near the border in order to destroy invading forces without creating extensive radioactive clouds; but the German farmers have consistently refused to have these weapons buried in their fields. The Nike Hercules is an anti-aircraft missile which is fired 150 miles into the air and creates nuclear explosions of one to twenty kilotons over high-flying bombers; but bombers now fly low to avoid radar, and the Nike Hercules is far less use than the much more accurate low-flying and conventionally armed missiles. For these reasons NATO has now withdrawn its atomic demolition mines and is in the process of dismantling its nuclear armed Nike Hercules.

Finally, as the Soviet Union responded in kind by deploying its own battlefield nuclear weapons, it became clear that any use by the West would be likely to trigger a response in kind, which would neutralise any advantage. In addition, the presence of intermediate nuclear weapons between strategic and battlefield weapons made it more likely that a use of nuclear weapons on the battlefield would escalate to a general nuclear war. To the extent that the likelihood of escalation increased, the likelihood of use decreased, and hence the value of battlefield weapons as an operational deterrent also decreased.

Decision-making about these battlefield nuclear weapons began to present some appalling problems. Because of the gravity of the decision to use battlefield nuclear weapons, the decision-making procedures were lengthened. For the weapons assigned to European NATO countries it became necessary for SACEUR to go through a three-phase consultation with the sixteen nation NATO Council before release could be authorised (although the use of nuclear weapons by the US forces in Europe could in theory bypass this procedure). In view of the urgency of release if the weapons were to be effective against advancing tanks, it began to seem unlikely that release would ever be authorised in time to be useful. The reaction of the other side to any move towards nuclear use would of course have to be taken into account. The nuclear warheads are now stored in special ammunition sites, all of which are of course well known to the Russians and under constant surveillance. If a decision was made to use nuclear weapons on the battlefield, then the first *observable* result would not be the use of nuclear weapons, but the movement of warheads from their storage sites. Such a move would immediately be detected by the other side. It is obvious that they would see the release of warheads as a highly threatening action, enormously strengthening the arguments for pre-emption and sabotage on their side.

Battlefield nuclear weapons naturally became a prime target for Russian military counter-measures, and plans to capture or destroy NATO nuclear weapons very early in any engagement became a predominant feature of Soviet military strategy. These plans force into sharp relief the 'use 'em or lose 'em' dilemma, the fear that NATO will be forced into premature nuclear release by the imminent loss of its means of nuclear escalation. Although normal peacetime procedures make such a prospect seem almost impossible to NATO's commanders, war has a nasty habit of creating its own confused and panicky dynamics that overwhelm the best laid peacetime schemes.

The longer intermediate range nuclear weapons have a rather different history from battlefield nuclear weapons. They are more closely associated with the task of linking the USA to Europe — the so-called 'umbrella' function. An underlying and persistent perception of Western Europeans is that of lying in the shadow of a Russian threat, on the edge of a vast and expandable military empire. In the crudest military terms, what West Europeans perceive is a possibility of 'selective nuclear blackmail'; in its more subtle form, it is suggested that a Europe consistently overshadowed by a vastly superior military power on its borders would inevitably in the long run find itself politically overshadowed or 'Finlandised'. This could be called ritualised dominance as opposed to ritualised equality. This perception is a very powerful force in favour of NATO nuclear presence in Europe, a presence which is not just part of a global superpower ritual. It is the intermediate range weapons which express this problem most vividly. So far as Western Europe is concerned, a very important constituent of the overhang is the nuclear weapons adapted to striking Western European targets, weapons which can travel anything from 100 to 500 kilometres, and can devastate at a stroke all major military installations in Europe — storage sites, ports, industrial centres, communications nodes, command headquarters. How then are these umbrella-ed powers to respond, as they see their own security diminishing in proportion to superpower progress in establishing a mutual nuclear veto?

Two ways of responding in military terms have now been tried in Western Europe, and both have been found to be 'No Through Roads'. One is for the umbrella-ed powers to acquire their own individual strategic nuclear deterrent, so that they set up their own self-cancelling 'assured dissuasion' against the opposing superpower. The other is to try to restore the fading superpower umbrella by 'tying in' the US strategic systems to European less-than-strategic systems, and trying to ensure that the USA will inevitably be drawn in to a European nuclear war whether she likes it or not. This is the doctrine associated with INF in Europe.

Both these options, while on the face of it having much to commend them, are in danger of being cures worse than the disease. Let us look briefly at each of them in turn.

The first option, that of countering the Soviet strategic deterrent with personalised strategic deterrents, has already been adopted to some degree by France and the UK. The problem of *extending* the French and British deterrent to cover Western Europe, however, is so fraught with political and military danger and difficulties that it cannot seriously be pursued. The British strategic deterrent, although assigned to NATO as required by the 1962 Nassau agreement, is always described by British officials as the UK weapon of the last resort, the 'ultimate guarantor of national security'. The French deterrent is quite specifically designed for national purposes only. The West Germans, for their part, have made it clear that they will not exchange a US guarantee for a British or French one. In any case, any nuclear umbrella extended from Britain or France over Germany would run into exactly the same conceptual problems as those which plague the idea of a US nuclear umbrella over Europe. How could the 'coupling' be secure? Would the UK commit suicide for Germany?

Other suggestions for a different kind of nuclear deterrent are equally fraught with difficulties. Discussions about a European-wide multi-lateral force ran into insoluble problems of collaboration and control, of multiple manning and multiple vetoes, and there is no reason whatsoever to think that these difficulties would be any less if the issue were raised yet again. The basic problem is that a MAD strategic deterrent for Europe only makes sense with a unified decision-making centre (because nobody will commit suicide for anybody else), and that implies a United States or Europe far ahead of present political realities.

What about a German nuclear deterrent then? At first sight this might seem the best solution, since it is Germany that would be the first victim of a Soviet offensive. However, the West Germans are opposed to the possession of nuclear weapons, and the Soviet Union for its part would undoubtedly see an independent nuclear armed West Germany as a major threat to its security. Furthermore, the nuclear arming of West Germany on any significant scale would be an act of nuclear proliferation which would seriously damage the cause of nuclear arms control world-wide, and consequently reduce security rather than increase it.

Since the option of a European strategic deterrent was fraught with such dangers and difficulties, we seemed to be forced into the second option, that of 'tying-in' the US strategic nuclear system to less-than-strategic nuclear weapons in Europe — the 'nuclear linkage' idea which justified the Cruise and Pershing II deployments in Europe.

The Symbolic Link

Out of all this confusion a new light is now beginning to dawn, and a new consensus is beginning to form.

There is one kind of linkage between strategic nuclear weapons and conventional weapons which is now generally seen to be a mistake. That is the linkage which suggests that nuclear weapons are really no different from large conventional weapons; the idea that they are there just to back up conventional weapons, to fill gaps, as it were, in an independent conventional defence. At one time, for instance, it was NATO policy to use nuclear weapons operationally to destroy Soviet tanks once they had been channelled into 'killing grounds'. Such linkages are now seen to be without sense.

Behind this gap-filling operational use of nuclear weapons was the idea of extending the deterrent effect of nuclear weapons downwards by having a 'ladder of deterrence'. Nuclear weapons prevent war between nuclear powers, by so arranging things that any war is likely to lead to a major nuclear war. This is done by having a kind of ladder of weapons, with rungs — the lower rungs being quite 'ordinary' conventional weapons, like tanks and guns, and the top being huge nuclear weapons which can destroy whole cities at a blow. The risks at the top are so enormous that in theory no-one is going to set foot on the lower rungs, for fear of *escalation* — for fear, that is, that any military activity on the lower rungs may lead, whether by design or accident, to the unleashing of nuclear weapons. No one will start anything if they know that that is where it might finish.

A necessary part of the ladder idea is that there is a 'nuclear threshold' — a point at which conventional war will turn nuclear. The higher you go up, the nearer you are to this threshold — and the greater, therefore, the braking effect.

Ladder deterrence depends on making a credible threat to use nuclear weapons in war. They are at the top of the ladder, and if they cannot be as it were 'fused' by conventional war, then it is believed by those with a ladder image that they lose all their deterrent effect — they become, in fact irrelevant to operational defence.

There is, of course, a fundamental difficulty about this image. Nearly everyone accepts that nuclear weapons are in fact rationally unusable. This has been true ever since the Soviet Union acquired a substantial nuclear capability in the 1960s, and it is even more true now that the nuclear winter has emerged as a serious possibility. How then can we rationally threaten to carry out an irrational action?

The answer is, of course, that you can't — but you can *irrationally* threaten to carry out an irrational action. Ladder deterrence then means that you have to pretend to be a bit mad — to pretend that in conventional war you would at some point start using nuclear weapons, even although it would be suicidal to do so. This could indeed work, just as the hijacker's threat can work, even though if he carried it out he would perish with everyone else in a plane crash. There is, however, a further problem hidden in this comparison. The mad hijacker depends on addressing a sane pilot. If the pilot is as mad as the hijacker, the threat will not work. Ladder deterrence therefore depends on saying to the potential enemy, 'We are mad — but we hope to God you are not!'

Of course the military reality is much more subtle than this caricature suggests. It is not exactly that any particular *person* has to pretend to be mad. It is enough that there should be just enough *uncertainty* and *insecurity* built into the system so that the enemy will fear that you *might* 'go nuclear', hence the whole mystique of 'uncertainty' developed by nuclear theorists. You have a number of different decision-making centres (France, UK, USA), and this helps to add to the uncertainty; you refuse to *define* the nuclear threshold, though you imply that it exists; you place your nuclear weapons in dangerous places, where they might unpredictably 'go off' in the early stages of a conventional war (for example, in Turkish mountain passes); or you so organise things so that escalation is automatic after a certain point — in other words, you delegate a madness function to a robot. Of course, there is a kind of 'mad' sense in all this; but there is also a great instability.

NATO's doctrine of 'flexible response', formally declared in 1967–68, had as its main purpose to improve conventional defence. Though it is now frequently associated with nuclear war-fighting ideas, it contained the germ of another approach to the nature of 'link' weapons — an approach which is now acquiring increasing momentum. One of the main purposes of flexible response was to get off the hook of NATO's old 'tripwire' doctrine of automatic nuclear response, which was losing all credibility. Its purpose was to create a 'decision-making space' between conventional weapons by having a very much more effective and usable *conventional* defence. While not rejecting the option of using nuclear weapons, it did contain an acknowledgement that they were *different in kind* from conventional weapons, and should be subject to a different decision-making process.

What is the nature of this 'difference in kind'? It is seen largely as a difference between operational weapons and 'political' weapons, or signalling weapons. This idea, that the 'link' nuclear weapons in Europe have a mainly *symbolic* or *political signalling* role, is steadily gaining acceptability among NATO decision-makers. This implies a contrast with operational use — the use of weapons in a primarily military role or to gain military advantage. What is the signal about? Clearly the signal is intended to link the battlefield situation with strategic nuclear weapons. The French have coined the term 'pre-strategic' to describe the proposed function of 'link' weapons. They are not primarily part of the war-fighting scene. They are conceived as a way of waving a red flag when France's 'vital interests' are threatened, giving an 'out of bounds' warning, pointing towards the ultimate peril of nuclear war, which is unfightable and unwinnable, pointing, therefore, towards the absolute necessity of a political resolution. At the same time, of course, the proposed symbolic function of nuclear weapons in Europe is meant to symbolise and express the other kind of linkage — the linkage of Western Europe with America.

While these link weapons are seen to point to 'MAD', they cannot be entirely separated from the battlefield situation if they are to be effective. They must, as it were, have a foot in both camps; they must have *some* operational significance. It would be no use at all, for instance, designating a link weapon to melt some ice on the North Pole. That would not be a link, it would just be a stunt. The link weapons, therefore, must have some definite military function.

This idea of the symbolic link which is gaining credibility in the West is not to be confused with 'ladder' deterrence, or with a kind of mechanical idea of deterrence in which nuclear weapons form a 'tripwire', or 'fill a gap', or 'trigger a holocaust'. All this is mechanistic thinking, not symbolic thinking, and with the mounting acceptance of the unwinnability of nuclear wars, it is symbolic thinking which is gaining ground.

Mechanical thinking actually destroys the meaning. A nuclear use which 'triggered' at a certain threshold is part of a machine response, a machine response which we have seen lacks all credibility. That is part of the sense behind NATO's cult of vagueness and uncertainty, the refusal to define; the nature of the link as a symbol depends on having 'decision-making space' around it.

There is a further dissimilarity between the mechanical 'ladder-type' deterrence and symbolic deterrence. Deterrence is potentially mutual — it can work for both sides simultaneously. This is not accidental. Ladder deterrence, however, must be one-sided; it cannot be reciprocal. Followed through to its logical conclusion, it must depend ultimately on posing a superior threat. In the ladder tradition no one is going to be content with being in a position to prevail at level five, knowing that his opponent can prevail at level six. To deter effectively, therefore, you must have what is called 'escalation dominance' — that is, you must be able to 'win' at every level, so that it is your *opponent* who is always forced to face the choice of moving up a rung, but deprived of any hope of winning higher up. There is no way, however, that *both* sides can be in this situation at the same time. Basically the ladder can only work if it is a way of maintaining superiority — and only one side can be king of the castle. That is why mechanical or ladder deterrence is a recipe for escalation. Symbolic deterrence, however, does not imply 'winning' nuclear wars at *any* level; rather it is a way of signalling 'no-win'.

In terms of perception, weapons which form a symbolic 'link' between MAD and effective conventional defence are a kind of catalyst, which join together and form a new compound which is not like either. MAD on its own has no roots in operational reality, and conventional defence on its own has no compelling deterrent effect against all war. The new MAD/[link]/CD compound, however, is perceived on the one hand as sharing the deterrent effect of the nuclear system, and on the other hand as sharing the 'usability' of conventional weapons. It is like a coin in which heads is MAD, tails is conventional defence and the link is the substance between. In a sense there is neither heads nor tails without the substance, and it is all heads or all tails according to your point of view.

This 'new compound' combines the opposites of military usability and military unusability, to create as it were a new rite, or new language of defence. It must be emphasised that this is simply a description of the way the situation is beginning to be perceived in the West at the present time. Since the strategic reality is constructed by perceptions, this is 'where we are', and it makes some sort of sense. Unless we can get hold of the kind of sense that it makes, we shall not find the way forward. Unless we understand where we are, we cannot know where to go from here. That is not to say that perceptions can't change; but, unless there is a veritable revolution, triggered for example by a major nuclear catastrophe, then it is highly probable that future perceptions will evolve from the present perceptions; and the positive meaning of the present is the raw material out of which we have to shape the future.

The Way Ahead

Having once understood the nature of the link, and the way it is commonly perceived, we can begin to see the kind of policy directions that make sense, if we want to participate in the historical process of creating new meanings out of old.

As regards less-than-strategic nuclear weapons, the questions we must ask are what kind of weapons do we need, how many, and where, in order to achieve the maximum symbolic and catalyst effect with the least risk and danger. Weapons are like other things people buy — if you don't really know what you want them for, you tend to get too many and usually the wrong kind. This is especially true when the military industrial complex is in the market place; the industrial part generating ever improved weaponry, and the military part tending to relapse into war-winning grooves. There is nothing fatalistic about this, however. The military industrial complex can be controlled if we know what we want. The tail does not have to wag the dog, if the dog is properly educated.

First of all, as long as NATO has weapons, it is important that it should retain firm control over them and always be in a position to make a proper and well-thought-out decision rather than be stampeded into a decision because of pressure of events. Nobody wants to see decisions delegated to a field commander or to have a rapid decision to use nuclear weapons forced by a collapsing conventional defence. Whatever we think about nuclear weapons, clearly we must agree with the view of the generals that deliberation about their use is better than desperation; and only deliberation can give to these weapons the symbolic and political meaning which they are intended to carry.

Some general guidelines for deployment or non-deployment follow from this principle. It seems sensible, for instance, to diminish reliance on very short-range nuclear systems, which are evidently more subject to 'use 'em or lose 'em' pressures which would certainly be there if large numbers of forward-based nuclear weapons were being overrun. This would have the added advantage of automatically releasing more artillery and back-up resources for a conventional role. It also seems sensible to reduce numbers and increase the security of those that are left. Use of nuclear weapons in thousands, or in hundreds, obviously makes no sense as a 'signal', but leads towards nuclear war-fighting and automatic escalation. At present, the argument used to support large numbers is that you have to be prepared to lose a lot (they are all fitted with self-destruct devices). There is a large attrition factor built in to the weapon deployment. It would, however, be less ambiguous and more clearly expressive of the 'signal' function to have fewer weapons more secure, and further back.

An even more important consequence of symbolic thinking is that any increase in effective conventional defence clearly implies an increase in the overall effectiveness of the symbolic deterrent. Because conventional defence is more credible, more effective, the immediate war-fighting relevance of the nuclear link is diminished, and space is provided for it to achieve its 'signalling' meaning. In the old 'ladder' concept there was a temptation to say that conventional defence should *not* be too good, so that nuclear response would be 'triggered' earlier. This was a bit like arguing for a bad conventional defence but littering the countryside with nuclear booby traps. With the new symbolic thinking about the 'link', however, the perception is growing that the better your conventional defence, the more credible and effective the nuclear signal. In mathematical terms, deterrence can be seen as a product of conventional defence and nuclear deterrence ($D = C \times N$).

The effect of the nuclear system in this concept, is pervasive — something like what McGeorge Bundy has called 'existential deterrence'; and the risk can diminish, even towards vanishing point, without the deterrence reality diminishing. The deterrent effect does not depend on a nuclear threshold; it does not depend on having a 'nuclear fuse' on the battlefield; it does not depend on filling gaps in conventional defence with nuclear weapons. The presence of nuclear weapons energises the whole system by a kind of electromagnetic effect.

This raises the important question of the future of intermediate range forces, such as Pershing II, Cruise missiles, and the SS20s, which we have lumped together with the short-range systems under the concept 'link weapons', since this is largely how they are perceived. If INF remain with us for some years, because of failure to achieve an early agreement, they too must be subjected to scrutiny in terms of their symbolic function. They are not to be seen as war-fighting weapons; they are not to be seen as first strike weapons or as 'decapitation' weapons (a serious problem with Pershing II, which can so rapidly reach Moscow). The last thing a signaller wants to do is to chop off the head of the person he is signalling to.

It may well be, however, that these intermediate range weapons are soon eliminated altogether on both sides, as both Mr Reagan and Mr Gorbachev have expressed a desire to achieve a 'zero option', and the negotiating gap appears to be bridgeable. It is the Europeans who are agitated about the 'breaking of links'. Yet it is not clear why they must have two different kinds of link (intermediate and tactical); this idea harks back to the old 'ladder deterrence' concept, with its potentially innumerable rungs. What is clear in the short term is that eliminating INF would focus much more attention on the link role of tactical nuclear weapons. It may well be that the eventual link would lie almost midway between the present two categories of short and intermediate range weapons — or that it should move out to sea.

At the beginning of chapter three I compared strategic nuclear weapons to the head of a dragon, and the less-than-strategic weapons to its body and tail, the tail being entwined with the Central Front in Europe. The best strategy may well be to tame the dragon rather than to seek to dismember it. As concepts and goals are clarified, and as it

becomes increasingly accepted in the East as in the West that the only rational objective is to avoid all war, so the possibilities of 'co-operative security' arrangements will open up, there will be many possibilities of 'trading asymmetries', reducing offensive elements of force postures and reducing ambiguities while maintaining defensive capability and mutual deterrence. It is very probable that link symbolism will continue to have a pervasive influence, especially on European perceptions.

None of this, however, is to be taken as unchangeable 'doctrine'. It may well be that the need for the link symbol fades rapidly as the superpower ritual becomes more formalised. Those who argue even now for a nuclear-free Europe tend to see strategic weapons as exercising an 'electromagnetic' effect in Europe without any physical link, and given certain political developments this could well become the dominant perception. This is, in fact, a different way of conceiving the linkage, rather than a way of dispensing with it.

There are no fixed and permanent policy guidelines. It is all too easy to polarise the debate about nuclear weapons into a 'good versus evil' conflict, in which diabolical motives are attributed by each side to the other. In reality, there is a powerful underlying consensus that it is war that must be conquered. We are like travellers lost in a wood, feeling our way forward. There is no map of the wood. There may be many alternative paths, and we do not know for sure where any path will lead until we have tried it: neither do we know what the wood will look like from further ahead, or what new paths will open up. The objective of the journey, however, is to get out of the wood; and getting out of the wood means leaving war behind us in the history of the human race; but to achieve this we have first to accept our history. This is the inescapable task of our generation.

5

The Rite of War

A favourite trick of human beings when confronted with a nasty problem is to pretend it does not exist. War is one of the problems that certainly does exist, and nuclear war in particular is a danger that will only come closer if we bury our heads in the sands.

There is one special way of pretending that war does not exist which is adopted by many would-be peacemakers. It is to say that war is 'evil'. That means you 'disown' it. It's nothing to do with you, but it's rather to do with all those *other* people who are subject to evil influences. The ideal way of dealing with evil is to find someone to blame — and then perhaps execute (or 're-educate') him, so that the source of the trouble ceases to exist. Perhaps it's the military who are 'to blame'; perhaps it's the politicians; or perhaps, if you are a female chauvinist, it's the men. 'Take the toys from the boys' — get rid of the military — remove the politicians — all is well. The mists of war will evaporate like a bad dream when a scapegoat is sacrificed, and the peace movement will inherit the earth. I don't believe a word of it. Moreover, I believe that this magical approach to the problem of war is based on a failure to come to grips with history, a failure to comprehend and accept our reality as a political and historical being and above all a disastrous failure to carry responsibility when the very survival of the human race depends on people accepting responsibility rather than discarding it.

Carrying responsibility does not mean feeling guilty either. That's just another kind of magic. If we decide we are all 'guilty' about war, then we might think the way out is to repent, and get rid of our 'guilty' parts. We can make our confessions, become pure in heart, and all will be well — Big Daddy will take care of history. He won't. Now is the time when the human race must come of age. And growing up means becoming *whole* — accepting the whole of what we are, the whole of

113

where we are, the whole of our group reality as well as our individual reality, the whole of our history as well as the whole of our present, the whole of our responsibility as political and historical beings with our feet on the earth and our minds reaching up towards a nobler future.

Accepting where we are is the first step in responsibility. We may not like where we are, but where we are is our raw material, like the clay on the potters' wheel. If we work at it, we may form a priceless work of art for future generations. If we fail, we may leave behind a sloppy mess. But we cannot walk away from this wheel. There is nowhere else to go.

The Roots of War

A common misunderstanding is to assume that war is caused by aggression, and aggression is evil. There are two mistakes here. Wars are not caused by aggression; aggression is not evil.

First of all, wars are not caused by aggression. War is a structural interaction between organised human groups. It cannot be 'reduced' to personal feelings, nor can it be properly comprehended in terms of personal feelings. Of course it *involves* personal feelings — even passions of a very high intensity. But we must get the causation right; it is not the feelings that cause the war, but the war that causes the feelings. I grew up hating Germans; but I did not know any. The war caused the feelings, not the feelings the war; and the war was related to political and military structures, and could only be understood at this level. In the same way, even in small groups like families, structural conflicts often have to be coped with on their own terms; it is not just a question of 'being nice'. When the structure is right, the feelings will fall into place.

People who do not understand this kind of cause and effect make some elementary mistakes. They think perhaps that the military must be very aggressive, when in fact the military are far less aggressive as a breed than businessmen, and the military on opposing sides often have a good deal of fellow feeling. They also may think that the structural conflict between East and West will go away if we only learn to be kind to each other — or that the arms race will stop because we have *détente*. It won't; as we discovered in the 1970s.

Neither is it helpful to say aggression is evil. On the contrary, aggression is one of the most universal characteristics of all animal species, and it is essential to survival. Aggression in its simplest form is to do with dispersing species through the available habitat; it is very closely related to flight, to which it is complementary. One animal threatens, the other withdraws, and so the species is distributed, just as negatively charged particles would distribute themselves around the surface of a sphere. Even the lowly amoeba knows how to flee.

Aggression, therefore, cannot be 'evil' unless we take a very jaundiced view of creation. An animal without the potential for aggression-and-flight is probably very sick, and is unlikely to survive.

There is, however, an important sense in which it is right to associate war with aggression. Warfare, or ritualised group aggression, fulfils for human groups the very same function which aggression in its simpler form fulfils for individuals. Warfare is to do with separation and dispersal, and through dispersal with *defining, maintaining, or expanding* the identity and viability of the group. Warfare is about group identity, and about the space within which identity is realised.

We must, however, beware of a reductionist interpretation of what a human group actually *is*. Human groups are essentially symbolic communities; man is by definition *Homo symbolicus*. He is a creature who lives in a world of symbols and meaning, just as a fish lives in water. Without communal symbols and meaning, man is no longer man, or woman woman. The identity of the human group which has to be maintained, defined, or extended by aggression is not therefore just the physical identity of an assembly of individuals, it is also, even among primitive peoples, a symbolic identity, an identity of meaning embodied in the culture, language and moral principles of the group.

Three Kinds of War

Warfare among primitive people can be divided into three main categories: *defensive* wars, *social* wars and wars of *expansion*.

The two first kinds of warfare, defensive and social wars, are practised to some degree by virtually all primitive human societies. Some tribes, at the extreme of unwarlikeness, embark on warfare only for the immediate defence of the group against attack. There is no military organisation, and tactics consist of a spontaneous use of

116   *The Rite of War*

methods and weapons employed in the hunt. Some tribes fight only in this way. The vast majority, however, also engage in social wars.

Social wars, as defined by Quincy Wright in his classic study of the subject, are wars fought for 'sport, ritual, revenge, personal prestige, or other *social* purposes'. Basically, all such wars are essentially a way of establishing a social relationship with another group — that is, they are aimed at establishing and defining the symbolic identity of one human group in relation to another. Societies which engage *only* in social wars of this kind are unlikely to have a special military group or class — though all boys are likely to have military training of some kind, and in many cases they embark on war as something of an adventure. Indeed, many primitive tribes engage in kinds of warfare which strongly resemble sports and which may have much to do with the origin of 'civilised' games.

Wars over women are common especially among tribes which practise 'exogamy' — the need to marry *outside* the community. This is not surprising, given the central importance of blood relationships which makes the community into a biological organism. It is at the contact points where the social organism has to define its boundaries or 'skin' that aggression is most likely to occur. The wars about women immortalised in the story of Helen of Troy have very deep roots in human prehistory. Wars of revenge are also common; and these nearly always follow the vengeance rule of 'an eye for an eye, and a tooth for a tooth'. This principle, which has been greatly misunderstood in the Christian tradition, is essentially a principle of damage limitation, a principle of balance. It is the symbolic re-establishment of an identity. It is *essentially* social, as are all wars in this second category — essentially, that is, to do with the *coexistence* of distinct human communities, and the definitions of relationships between them.

This is not true of the third category of war, *the war of expansion*, which is characteristic of the rise of civilisation.

Civilisation and Expansionism

Primitive communities are the 'base-line' human groups from which modern civilisations have developed. Whereas man has lived on the face of the earth for some three million years, civilisation as we use the word has only existed for seven thousand. Until then, the entire human population of the planet was probably less than that of a moderate sized city, and all of these lived in tribes or other groupings which we would call 'uncivilised' (i.e. un-town-ised), or primitive. Civilisation began about seven thousand years ago in the Nile Valley, giving rise to the culture of ancient Egypt, and later in the valley of the Indus in northern India, in the valley of the Yellow River in China, in Mesopotamia, and in Peru — but even so, these civilisations only affected a small proportion of the world's small human population, and even as recently as two thousand years ago, at the beginning of the Christian era, probably half the world's population was still 'primitive'.

In the last two thousand years, however, there has been an extraordinary and ever-accelerating change. Today we have nearly three *billion* human beings in the world — and less than 5 per cent of these are primitive, or in any way distinct from the vast galactic 'civilisations' which extend their tentacles across the face of the earth; and these 5 per cent are rapidly being 'civilised' — i.e. 'tidied up', assimilated, and deprived of autonomy — or eliminated. In massive metamorphoses of planetary society war has played a crucial role. It is worth taking a closer look at the ignition phase and the boost phase of this process.

In primitive societies, before writing, the outreach of a human community in *time and space* was limited. Communication and influence could only extend by word of mouth and face-to-face contacts, and distance runners were used for communication. History was identical with folk memory and myth, passed on by oral tradition. Communities were grouped in clusters of families with a blood relationship forming a 'village'. Beyond that was the tribe, which might include a number of villages. The tribe here-and-now *was* the entire community, and the entire community *was* the tribe. This was the group identity which had to be maintained if necessary by defensive and social wars.

The next development after hunter-gathering was herding and cultivating. Herdsmen kept their animals and bred them instead of chasing after them; and agriculturists planted crops they wanted to eat instead of just taking what came. Such cultures generally differ from hunter-gatherer societies in a number of important aspects. They have a different relationship to the land, and to tribal territory. Pre-agricultural hunter-gatherers are often fairly mobile, and are able to exploit a wide territory without fixed boundaries. Like the original American Indians, they tend to feel 'at one' with the forests and the sea, but they do not 'own' them. Agriculturalists, however, and to a lesser extent herdsmen, cannot be mobile or flexible in the same way. They invest their labour in a particular patch of land, which then becomes part of them and part of the community in a different sense, and the idea of owning and defending *territory*, therefore, comes much more to the fore.

At the same time, agricultural and pastoral communities can become quite large. Whereas hunter-gatherer communities are typically of village size, or 'tribes' of village-sized communities, agricultural and pastoral communities commonly involve large tribal groups and federations of tribes which approach our concept of a 'state'. As societies expand in size, so there is an increasing degree of specialisation between different groups in society. Among hunter-gatherers the general rule is that everyone has to produce food (usually the men hunt and the women gather), but with the advance of agriculture and herding, and the production of surplus food in the ownership of the group, many kinds of specialisation become possible. There can be classes of priests, metal-workers, soldiers. There is often a centralised political authority usually taking the form of a ritual kingship. Together with this class specialisation a considerable degree of hierarchy frequently develops, and we find 'stratified' societies, with layers of people one on top of the other, and a priest/king at the summit of a pyramid.

This is the 'take-off' point for most advanced cultures and civilisations. It is also the take-off point for wars of expansion.

Wars of Expansion

As communities become larger, socially more stratified and more advanced in agricultural and herding techniques, so they practise more of the third type of war, the war of expansion. These have been classified by Quincy Wright as *economic* and *political* wars. They are wars embarked upon for the purpose of acquiring slaves, cattle pastures, agricultural lands, or other economic assets essential to the life of the group, or to maintain in power a ruling class, or to expand the area of political control.

Of course 'take-off' communities have also far more defensive wars than pre-take-off communities. Physical territory was always an important aspect of social identity. As societies expand and establish a fixed territorial base, required by agriculture and some forms of herding, so their territorial identity becomes both *larger* and more *vulnerable*, or brittle. There are more points at which its physical identity can be threatened, and flight is not an option. (Most hunter-gatherers much prefer flight to fight if the option is open.) Defensive military organisation therefore becomes important.

The new war dynamic which is ignited in the 'boost phase' of many civilisations, however, is not just defensive, or just social. As primitive societies grow into larger and more complex social organisations, they *must feed upon* other human communities. Like individuals, they can only grow by eating. More people are needed, more territory is needed. Expanding primitive cultures therefore have to develop a *digestive system*. Hunter-gatherer communities with their informal, flexible and largely a-political relationships have virtually no digestive systems — no means of devouring each other as communities. The development of *pyramid-shaped* societies with specialised classes increases the potential for large-scale organisation and development, extending outwards in space, and these very same hierarchies and pyramids constitute the digestive systems which enable these societies to absorb others. The most common form in which this digesting takes place is through conquest.

In this expansive process by which dynamic human cultures absorb their neighbours, warfare conducted by organised military forces has usually played a vital role. The purpose of those wars, therefore, is not just to define and preserve the identity of the group, but to expand that identity. The military are the 'limbs, claws and teeth' — i.e. they are concerned with pursuing, subduing, and if necessary destroying the enemy. Digestion begins in the mouth (though it does not end there). For very fundamental biological and physical reasons, developments in the tools and organisation of war tend in the early phase of civilisation to greatly increase the offensive potential of a well-organised military power, and make resistance less feasible.

RW-I

To a large extent, the modern 'nation states' of which we are now so proud were hammered out on an anvil of war. England has been 'eaten' three or four times over — by the Anglo-Saxons, the Danes, the Normans — though after that we became somewhat indigestible. It would be a great mistake, however, to describe this process by which super-societies were formed *only* in terms of conquest and submission. The other component of the social superglue, *charismatic* cohesion, the attractive force of the superdominant conqueror was at least of equal importance. As primitive societies grow, develop, acquire central institutions, wealth, kingship, pomp and circumstance, so they exercise a hypnotic and attractive force on neighbouring communities. As systems of communication extend outwards, so this attractive force extends, exercising a kind of gravitational pull towards the centre. Through cultural absorption and imitation, growing civilisations extend their territory outwards, while through 'succession' rituals the charisma is passed on, and so communities extend in time as well as in space.

It is through this kind of organic process that the human race has reached its present degree of conflict and cohesion.

War and Ritual

Ritualisation, which means making a 'rite' or ritual of an action, is a term which is now widely used in the study of both human and animal behaviour. It implies that some particular action or aspect of behaviour — like eating, drinking, fighting — is given a formal structure, follows a set of rules, and acquires a wider meaning than the original action. The wider meaning can then become dominant, and can completely absorb the original meaning or function.

The antlers of stags are a good example of how biological structures are 'ritualised'. The stag carries on either side of its skull a small tree of bones which can be very much heavier than the skull which carries them. The 'original' function of spikes or horns on the heads of animals is presumably to do damage to other animals. They are, therefore, part of the 'aggressive' behaviour complex. Now one primary function of aggression as between individuals within a species is to 'select' dominant animals for leading positions through fighting, or 'competition'. This particular function of aggression has played an important part in the evolution of the stags' antlers. They play a very important part in 'ritualised' fighting for mates, when competing stags lock antlers and wrestle.

However, the ritual meaning of the antlers has moved very far from the original function of spikes on the head. So far, in fact, that these complicated bony structures are extremely inefficient as weapons. They are far too big, heavy and complicated — and they are not even sharp. It is now their ritual meaning which is biologically dominant rather than their original function.

There are plenty of analogues to this kind of development in human cultural 'evolution'. The mace, for instance, is now primarily under-stood and accepted as a symbol of authority. In the British House of Lords, for instance, the Lord Chancellor sits on his 'woolsack' (itself a symbol of wealth) with his golden mace in front of him. If we trace the mace back through history, however, we find that it is in fact a weapon — a weapon of a rather primitive and gruesome kind, consisting of a heavy metal ball, often with spikes on, attached to a pole, and well adapted to crushing human skulls. It is, however, not expected that the Lord Chancellor will use his mace in this way to impose his authority on his 'peers'.

If this seems a frivolous example, it would seem much less frivolous to someone who had seen what a mace can do to a man's head.

The process of ritualisation, of creating 'new meanings out of old', is not, however, just something to do with high ceremonial. Creating new meanings out of old is what human cultural evolution is all about. Old meanings are always there as our 'raw material' — like the potter's clay. Without them, we have no material, and can therefore create nothing. Yet without the firm and sensitive hands of the potter, the clay crumbles into useless fragments or collapses into a sticky mess.

What we can see in both these examples, the biological evolution of the stag's antlers and the cultural evolution of the Chancellor's mace, is that history involves a continuous modification of meaning. The past meaning is in a sense the 'raw material' of the present meaning, just as the present is the raw material of the future, though none of the material of history is 'raw', since it all carries meaning. The same is true of our individual lives; they are unfinished stories, the meaning of which is still open. The *past* is not a closed book. It is still open, since its meaning awaits completion in the present and in the future.

Ambiguities are therefore opportunities. In the present superpower confrontation, we have an ambiguity which could spell disaster or salvation. Both meanings are present and vying for supremacy. As we have seen in Chapter 1, there is a profound ambiguity of defence and offence in the postures of the opposing powers. This ambiguity is a *real* ambiguity — it is not an ambiguity which can somehow instantly be resolved by getting more information; we can only resolve it by participating in history.

Ritualisation, whether biological or cultural, gives us the clue we need. The whole history of human warfare is in a sense consummated and encapsulated in present East–West confrontation. Defensive wars, social wars, wars of expansion are all contained and expressed in this confrontation. We cannot just discard this history. We can recycle the old meanings, and find a way of making much better sense. We cannot, however, wait for thousands of years of biological evolution to do this for us or even for hundreds of years of cultural evolution to do it for us. We have now to take possession of our histories in a totally new way, and with a much shorter time space. We have to do a lot of growing up in a very short time.

New Meanings Out of Old

What are the meanings from the past which we seek to develop?

First of all, of the three basic traditions of war we have identified, *defensive war* is both the most ancient and the best understood. It is also the only form of war that is most fully legitimised, both in international law (under stringent conditions) and in the moral attitudes and beliefs of the people. Very few would deny an individual or a state the right to fight to preserve its own integrity.

It appears that, at the conventional level, we are now reaching a stage when effective defence is possible in a fairly 'pure' form — a defence which is quite unambiguously 'just defence' or *just* for 'defence'. Because of the advances in transparency, in anti-tank and anti-air systems, in armour penetration technology, in barrier formation, it could well become very difficult for one technologically advanced nation to invade another by overt military action. The West is well

placed with its vast resources, technological lead and moral commitment, to pioneer a form of defence, beginning in Central Europe, which
will perfect and consummate the tradition of defensive war — perfect it
to such an extent that such war *in practice* becomes obsolete, being
gradually replaced by the concept of defensive deterrence. Effective
defensive deterrence as a generalised military doctrine implies the
termination of war in practice, but the continuation of war as ritual.

It would, however, be quite wrong to think of this ritualisation as a
'technological fix', which somehow freezes history by imposing a
mechanical solution to the problem of war. This is no such fix. There
are new meanings to be drawn out of old — but, as always, it is the
meaning that matters. War has never been intelligible purely in terms of
hardware and military doctrine. Conquest and defeat have always had a
high symbolic content, and their causes lie deep in the human psyche.
Defensive deterrence, therefore, also has primarily to express determination, cohesion, will, moral commitment.

The ritual of defensive war-gaming must first be rooted firmly in
military reality. It could take the form, for instance of preparation for
the effective operational defence of Western Europe, as described in
Chapter 2. As the defence-only meaning becomes institutionalised,
however, the ritual element will come to predominate over the military.
The threat will diminish; the determination not to succumb to force will
be properly expressed in ritual form. The Soviet Union, assured that no
offensive from the East could succeed, but also that no offensive from
the West is contemplated, could eventually follow suit with a more
unambiguously defensive posture, which nevertheless vigorously expressed in military form its determination that the Russian homeland
should never again be invaded from the West. If this meaning were
expressed both in defence postures and in co-operative confidence-
building regimes, then the ritual of 'mutual security' would begin to
take shape.

The nuclear system presents quite another challenge. Nuclear
deterrence depends not on defence, but on balancing offence against
offence. In mutual deterrence the opposing threats cancel each other
out. To be stable, such a system requires an assured deterrent on both
sides. Nuclear weapons are already in rational terms a deterrent against
each other — in fact they are many times over a total deterrent. Yet in

spite of the superfluity of weapons, the numbers game between the superpowers remains of supreme importance. Why is this so?

Part of the reason is the drift towards first strike which we described in Chapter 3. Equally important, however, is the *already ritualised* meaning of the 'nuclear balance'. In the 1950s the Soviet Union, only a generation after it had left the Middle Ages by a bloody revolution, with its economy and population decimated by war, embarked on a competition in nuclear weapons with the most advanced and super-dominant industrial nation in the world — a competition in which the opposition already had a head start. In 1972, in the SALT I accords, both nations agreed to call it a draw; the USA formally acknowledged that the Soviet Union had achieved 'parity'; and, what's more, both sides agreed that parity must henceforth be the basic rule which regulated all nuclear arms agreements to be concluded between them. It is hardly surprising that for the Soviet Union this was a supreme achievement which immeasurably bolstered both their self-image and their status in the eyes of the rest of the world. Whatever they have done in practice since that time, neither side has ever since deviated in theory from the principle of equality.

Accepting the principle of equality in offensive arms means two things. First of all, it means that those arms are *not to fight with*. You don't fight unless you think you can win, and if the enemy has the same offensive potential as you — and you have agreed in treaty form that this should be the case — then clearly neither side intends to fight. This situation is true of all offensive weapons, but is infinitely reinforced by the superstructure of nuclear arsenals. Agreeing about equality in weapons of this kind therefore means agreeing that they are not weapons; agreeing on the new meaning implies discarding the old. This is the ritualisation which the SALT I accords tried to achieve — however inadequately. Although they are not weapons, the nuclear arsenals remain crucially important symbols — symbolic of equality, but also in a strange way symbols of mutual dependence. They have become, in fact, the arch-status symbols — the culmination of the ancient tradition of *social wars*, by which communities express and define a relationship with each other.

By defining their relationships with each other, they also define themselves. Each side in its rhetoric portrays itself as an army of light fighting against an army of darkness; but in a sense the light needs the darkness as its foil. If you were to deprive either side of the stereotype enemy, the task of reconstructing a viable self-image would be virtually impossible. There is, therefore, at a deeper level, a kind of need *not* to win totally, which is also expressed and ritualised in the nuclear balance. It is essential to take co-operative security seriously, since this tradition, in spite of all the failures of the past, must play an important part in the process of ritualisation by which weapons are gradually transformed into non-weapons.

Co-operative security, which includes all kinds of negotiations and treaties between antagonists, must *not* be seen just as a means of being friendly instead of hostile — a woolly-minded kind of *détente*. Co-operative security is also a way of managing and even conducting antagonistic relationships. Arms control treaties and confidence-building measures can form the elements of a new language; they make new meanings possible. Once a certain 'confidence-building measure' is defined, then it is part of a new language or a new 'game', *even if the rules are not kept*. Breaking the rules is quite different from having no rules to break. Many of our highly formalised 'games' (such as fencing) have in fact evolved from combat and warfare — which is one reason why they are sometimes so highly charged in terms of group rivalries.

Clausewitz said that war was the continuation of politics by (or with the help of) 'other means'. We have to strive to contain the phenomenon of war within the game of international politics. The elaboration of systems of co-operative security is essential to this process. There are three tasks we must achieve in relation to nuclear weapons in order to rid the world of the peril of war. It is a new form of the 'three Rs' — Ritualise, Reduce, and Remove. The first 'R' is the key.

What, then, of the third tradition of war which we have identified — the expansionist or empire-building wars, which have been the primary means by which human cultures have up to now extended tentacles around the surface of the globe?

In a sense, we can see the present military confrontation between the superpowers as the grand finale in the history of military empire. The Soviet Union is a vast military empire, in the sense that it has established and maintains supremacy over a large and diverse collection of peoples in part through the use or threat of military force, just as

England did until a generation ago, and just as Napoleon did, and Venice did, and Charlemagne did, and Egypt did, and so on into the mists of history.

Many would argue that the USA by the same definition also has some characteristics of empire. We can make such judgements of fact without making any judgements of value. We may on balance, lukewarmly, or even passionately, believe in the moral superiority of our system and yet acknowledge that at one level we are talking about a clash of empires. Again, there is a wide divergence of view about the extent to which the West in recent years has simply reacted to Soviet military expansion, and the extent to which it has itself shown expansionist tendencies, and the East has reacted. As we saw in Chapter 1, history is still ambiguous about this matter. The meaning of the past has yet to be completed in the future.

There is, however, nothing evil about expanding empires as such. The English should be the last to take up such a position. Much more important is what kind of identity they are seeking to expand. This brings us to the great dilemma of military power in our generation, a dilemma which is now faced by both East and West. It arises from the contradiction between the military identity and the symbolic meaning which constitutes our real identity.

The contradiction in Western culture goes back at least to the time when the empire builder Jesus Christ told his supporter Peter in AD 32 to 'put up his sword, because he who takes the sword shall perish by the sword'. This did not, of course, prevent the followers of Christ from establishing military empires in His name for the next two thousand years. However, it did insert an element of discomfort into the body politic of Christendom, rather like the piece of grit in the oyster which generates the pearl.

The positive meaning which attaches to this piece of grit is that there are values essential to our identity which cannot satisfactorily be advanced by killing people — or, at the mythological level, by killing the enemy. The expression in history of these values is essentially the tradition of human rights, which has been gathering momentum throughout all the great historic revolutionary movements — English, American, French, Russian, and Chinese — even when these revolutions made full use of the sword (or the guillotine) to drive home the point. The tradition derives quite directly from the teaching of Jesus that there are no 'aliens': that human beings constitute one family, that all are free, all are equal. The American constitution, building on this tradition, was even able to declare, in the face of all experience and common sense, that it was self-evident that all men were born equal — endowed by their Maker with certain inalienable rights. Of course America went on digesting Indians and Africans just the same. But the problems of indigestion were building up — aggravated by the new symbolic identity.

Human Solidarity

The First and Second Articles of the Universal Declaration of Human Rights repeat the creed that 'All human beings are born free and equal in dignity and rights'. This statement can easily be assailed philosophic-ally as neither self-evidently true nor even comprehensible. Yet it is the foundation of all that follows. It is basically an *option* — a stance we take up, not at random, but because at a level deeper than that of rationality we sense that it is right. If anyone rejects or ridicules this stance, the dispute cannot be resolved by rational debate alone.

It is astonishing that this statement is enshrined as a universal principle in a document which has received the formal assent of representatives of virtually the entire population of the world. The principle implies decisive rejection of totalitarianism, which confers on collectives or specific groups rights of control and domination over others. Social and political systems have been built and are still built on this contrary assumption, sometimes explicit and sometimes implicit. It may be that in the long-term perspective mankind is at a point where the basic option has to be taken up once and for all, and it is an opinion which cuts right across traditional political alignments of right and left.

These rights which are proclaimed in the Universal Declaration have been divided into two categories in subsequent documents: *economic and social* rights like work, food and education, are distinguished from *civil and political* rights which are to do with freedom and political organisation. On the whole, the Western nations use the term human rights to refer to freedom rights, or civil and political rights, and the Communist countries use the term to refer to justice rights, which are more of an economic and social nature. Western nations therefore tend to use the term human rights as a stick to beat Communists, pointing to abuse of freedom in Communist countries, and the Communist countries use their version of human rights as a stick to beat the capitalist nations, pointing to unemployment, bad housing and poverty. Clearly there is no future in limiting the term human rights to one or the other side in this debate. Both sides are resoundingly and undeniably right, and each side can legitimately base its case on documents solemnly ratified by both. Justice rights and freedom rights cannot be separated. A vote is no use to a starving man: but a feast in prison is no answer to political persecution.

Self-determination

Closely linked to the tradition of human rights, around which the symbolic identity of the West is constituted, is the tradition of *self-determination* — the belief that every people has a right to choose and establish its own way of life and its own form of government without forcible intervention from outside.

This is also a principle which now has unshakeable foundations in international law. There is no way in which any modern state on the world stage can deny the principle of self-determination. Intervention must always be justified on the basis of that principle — if you invade another country it must be because they are threatened and ask for help — or perhaps because the people have not *freely* chosen, and need liberating. Hypocrisy maybe; but, as I have said earlier, hypocrisy is the tribute paid by vice to virtue, and it is precisely out of such hypocrisy that codes of behaviour eventually emerge.

The conflict between the tradition of self-determination and the tradition of military empires is clear. What you can never claim overtly is that you intervene militarily to maintain or extend your own empire, however desirable that may be; and yet the dynamics of military power force you to intervene precisely for those reasons which you hotly deny.

This is not just the old problem of a conflict between militarism and idealism. That is a false antithesis. The doctrine of self-determination itself emerged from conflict and real-politics; and is still rooted in conflict. Again, all I said earlier, in World War I, and at the Treaty of

Versailles which concluded it, the victorious allies gave the principle of self-determination a great boost because they saw it as an ideal way of helping to disintegrate the Austro-Hungarian empire, by allying themselves with subject people. They did not expect the principle to backfire and destroy the British and French empires, but it did. Principles of this kind have a habit of biting the hand that feeds them. The principle of self-determination has been established because people were prepared to fight for liberation; but it is also true the other way round — they were prepared to fight because they were fighting for a principle.

Within our Western democratic societies, we are able to replace leaders through the ritual of the ballot box. This is a colossal achievement which we should never underestimate, and it is essentially a ritualisation of revolution. So fully is the process ritualised, that the idea of a defeated candidate marching against the White House, or besieging No. 10 Downing Street, is absurd. In the Philippines, however, at the time of writing (1986), the connection between revolution and the ballot box, between justice and the will to resist, is much nearer the surface. The guiding principles of international law do not come down from heaven on tablets of stone. They arise like a fine distillation from the cauldron of politics.

So closely bound is the West now and for good or ill to the tradition of human rights and the self-determination of peoples, that to deny this tradition is to destroy the very identity which is being defended. And this has military consequences. If there is no shared meaning behind military policy, if it is not based on shared beliefs and aspirations, then it won't work as a military policy. Funds will not be voted by congress for the President's war aims; conscription will be refused (as it already is by a significant proportion of West Germans, and by a dramatically increasing number of East Germans, who are choosing prison as an alternative). Alliances will fall apart, the people will not be prepared to fight for an unjust cause. When morals go, morale goes too. That is how wars are lost, and therefore how deterrence will fail.

For the Soviet Union, the problem is less acute, and precisely because the core values of freedom and self-determination are there less advanced. There is still a very substantial consensus about military policy within the Soviet Union. Information is controlled, dissent is suppressed, the people believe that their military policy is entirely one of response to threat, and the memory of 20 million dead in the last war is still kept fresh. The military threat from the West helps to maintain the coherence of the Soviet military empire, and greatly strengthens the legitimacy of the military élite. Nevertheless, there are tensions in the Soviet Union also between moral identity and military policy. Soviet conscripts who have served in Afghanistan and taken part in total village executions do not easily reconcile these with the brotherhood of the proletariat. Soviet occupying forces in East Germany, Czecho-slovakia and Poland are well aware of the hostility of the people, and cannot by any mental gymnastics see themselves as liberators, or as maintaining the principle of self-determination. Yet the Soviet Union is committed to such a principle, not only as a signatory of the UN Charter, but also in its own constitution which allows a right of secession — even to the member states of the USSR.

The third tradition of war, that of expanding empire, is therefore, beginning to suffer from severe internal stresses and strains because of the conflict between military empire and symbolic identity. At the very same time, by providential coincidence, wars of expansion are becoming obsolete for purely military reasons, since effective conventional defence becomes possible at the conventional level, and an effective stalemate is formalised in nuclear weapons. What is the meaning of this changing situation?

A New Birth

The force of the right of self-determination, and of the whole structure of human rights associated with it, is the moral equivalent of the hydrogen bomb; and like the hydrogen bomb, it cannot be dismantled. Once the genie is out of the bottle, it is impossible to put it back. Even if it is temporarily suppressed, it can always be reinvented — and it surely will be. The spiritual force behind this principle is potentially infinitely greater than any spiritual force which can be evoked for the support of capitalism in any of its present forms, or of socialism in any of its present forms. It is a principle which has a much deeper source in history and in the human psyche and which will continue to energise the human race for countless generations, long after the conflict between capitalism and socialism has found its place in the yellowing pages of history.

The new human identity which is struggling to be born has to come out of the present, in all its historical earthiness, complexity and ambiguity. It is we in this generation who are in a sense the mother, the baby — and the midwife. The world is in labour and the pain could herald a new birth, but it is our responsibility to see that the birth is successful.

How can such good come out of such evil? How can human solidarity be enhanced by threats of genocide? How can human rights be advanced by military imperialism? How can humanity be transformed by nuclear weapons?

If we begin with a belief that there is an evil god warring with a good god, for control of the universe, then clearly these questions are unanswerable. There is, however, at the root of Judaeo-Christianity a deeper intuition, and one that is shared by the mystical traditions of East and West alike. It is that there is only one God, and that 'All manner of things shall be well'.

If the military confrontation which now threatens us with extinction were nothing else but the summation of all that is seen as 'evil' and 'alien' in man, nothing but violence, hatred and oppression writ large, the projection of diabolic forces in the world stage, then clearly nothing but protest or conversion can be justified.

This is, however, not the case. The new meanings are already enshrined in the old, like the kernel in the nut. The right of self-defence is itself an expression of the right of self-determination, and the right of self-defence exists because it has been 'claimed'. The military reality must now be brought increasingly into accord with this right. That is why defence has to become 'just defence'. At the nuclear level, the same meaning is expressed in another form. The age of winning wars is drawing to a close. If we wish to build empires which express our true identities, they have to be empires of a new kind, empires 'not of this world'.

The new meanings, however, are only there 'in potency', to use the language of the mediaeval philosophy; it is we who have to make them 'actual'. We can make the new meanings actual by ritualising the old. To ritualise is not to reject; nor is it to accept; it is to transform. We have to transform the rite of war into the rite of human solidarity. As we approach the threshold of the third millennium, the consciousness of human solidarity is rising rapidly. It is our task in this generation to raise ourselves to a higher level in our evolutionary climb.

The words of the prophet Isaiah should be for us at once a great hope, a great reality, and an inspiration to action:

> And they shall repair the waste cities, the desolations
>   of many generations,
> Violence shall be no more heard in thy land,
> Wasting nor destruction within thy borders;
> But thou shalt call thy walls salvation,
> And thy gates praise.   (Isa. 60: 18)